THE
LORE OF THE
LAND

The
Goodlife
Press

THE LORE OF THE LAND

By John Seymour
with illustrations by Sally Seymour

First published in 1982 by Whittet Books Ltd.
Text © 1982 John Seymour, 2012 Anne Sears
Illustrations © 1982, 2012 Sally Seymour

This 2012 edition is published by The Good Life Press Ltd.
ISBN 978-1-907866-05-0

A CIP catalogue record for this book is available from the British
Library.

Printed and bound in Bodmin, Cornwall by MPG Books Ltd.

Contents

sainfoin

Chapter 4 Walls, Hedges, Fences and Gates with a Short Word on Roads and Paths 76-99

Chapter 5 Woodland 100-110

Chapter 6 Trees 111-163

Chapter 7 Ponds and Lakes 164-182

Index 183

The author of the words dedicates

them to the illustrator

Foreword

I have always used this book for reference when needed, but for the first time I have read it from cover to cover. Why would I normally want to read about how to work out how far a tree would reach when felled, or how to tap an artesian spring, or make a gate from riven ash, unless I was about to embark upon that task? However, as I read on, I realised that The Lore of the Land is more than a practical text book. It is a celebration of good country practises. It is a pleasure to read just for the satisfaction of learning about a working system developed in the most practical and effective way over hundreds of years of land husbandry. This book is full of knowledge and wisdom of great importance. It is a succession of wonderful realisations about how and why these methods were developed, and why they must not be lost.

It is written in my father's inimitable style – full of his fine outspoken opinions which might enrage or amuse, but to me everything makes such beautiful sense. His attitude towards the land is one of respect and responsibility, the message being that there is room for all life on this planet, give or take a little jostling for position here and there. He shows how we have worked out methods of making the land sweeter and more able to grow the food that we flourish on without unduly disturbing the balance of nature. There is an art to working with what we have, using materials around us with ingenuity and skill, and sensitivity.

Through his own experience John captures and makes accessible a way of life lived before heavy machinery, poisonous chemicals, oil-based fertilizers and an attitude of destruction were in common use on the land. He shows us that there is no reason on earth to poison and destroy for our food, for in doing so the food is unhealthy, and those methods ultimately cannot sustain the land we depend on.

I am witness to John having tackled the difficulties of working our farm in Pembrokeshire. Part of the land was pure sand, and some an acid clay sump to the surrounding hills, with its broken down walls and not a fence in sight. As a child I watched him splitting ash for gates, and putting up miles of fencing, planting hundreds of trees and draining fields that had previously swallowed tractors and live-stock. This was all done on a shoestring and mostly by his, and visitors', graft using spades and other hand tools. He never baulked at physical work, even when he was 90, and had moved back here to live with us. At that great age he helped to dig a pit 10' x 6' x 4' for a composting tank for the lavatory, and plant an orchard of fruit trees in which he wanted to be buried. He worked as hard as anyone 40 years younger. He had always found a sense of peace and spirituality in the act of using his strength and enthusiasm to work alongside nature.

This book is a treasure. It marries John's practical philosophy and knowledge, with my mother's beautiful illustrations and clear diagrams. It is a testament to their enduring friendship and wonderful working relationship, even though they had lived apart for some years. John's strong voice, Sally's distinctive artwork and the fact that they were both passionate about the philosophy of life they had developed together have made a book that I will always cherish.

As John said, "Live simply with nature and find pleasure, comfort and true civilization in simple things".

Anne Sears, April 2012
www.carninglipress.co.uk

Footnote:

This book was written in the early 80s and, therefore, I would urge readers to employ the author's principle of OMCS (Old Mother Common Sense) and make allowances for some of the 'new' technologies referred to and terminologies used. Also please don't attempt to boil creosote – I was there and it was spectacular!

Introduction

The 'owner' of a piece of land has an enormous responsibility, whether the piece is large or small. The very word 'owner' is a misnomer when applied to land. The robin that hops about your garden, and the worms that he hunts, are, in their own terms, just as much 'owners' of the land they occupy as you are. 'Trustee' would be a better word. Anyone who comes into possession, in human terms, of a piece of land, should look upon himself or herself as the trustee of that piece of land – the 'husbandman' – responsible for increasing the sum of living things on that land, holding the land just as much for the benefit of the robin, the wren and the earthworm, even the bacteria in the soil, as for himself.

Of course we have a right to use the land for our own purposes, to grow food, for example, or timber, or to make it beautiful to our eyes. We have a right – and a duty – to maintain a due order and balance among all the other forms of life on it. Man is part of Nature too and must take his part in the dance of Life and also of Death. If the caterpillars destroy our cabbages we have a right to sort 'em out. We do *not* have a right, though, to sort 'em out by using some indiscriminate poison that is going to do all other kinds of living things to death.

As well as rights, we have a positive duty with regard to land. According to the Book of Genesis, God put the Man and the Woman in the Garden to 'dress it and keep it'. Whether we look upon Genesis as divinely inspired or not, it is obvious that we should do just this. We should hand the land on to the next trustee better, more fruitful, more beautiful, and richer in living creatures than it was when we took it over. The trusteeship of land is a daunting responsibility. It is part of the Earth's surface that we are given charge of, full of living creatures other than mankind, in trust for future generations of humans as well as all forms of life.

The reason why our land is so desperately badly husbanded now is that it is held in too large units. The loving care that a good husbandman can devote to a piece of land can only be spread so far; when one person 'owns' hundreds of acres he is forced to resort to mechanical and chemical warfare; the bulldozer and the poison spray take the place of Adam's spade and Eve's pruning shears. I am not inveighing against chemicals and machinery but simply against the thoughtless abuse of these things made necessary by over-swollen land holdings. It can be seen over and over again that a smallholding is more fruitful, more beautiful, and richer in varied life than a vast agribusiness. This book is not intended for the agribusinessman, but for the holder of a piece of land of a size that he can really husband and cope with, and treat with the tender loving care that we should always give to the soil and its denizens. Neither does this book tell people how to grow food: there are plenty of good books on that subject. It is to exhort people to care well and humanely for the land in their charge, to show how it is possible to tend the land beautifully: to plant it with trees, to establish well cared-for hedges instead of wire fences, to build good timber gates instead of buying steel ones that quickly rust and become eye-sores, to drain wet places where drainage is needed and to do all the other operations that generally come under the heading of 'estate management' when applied to huge estates. If the 'estate management' side of things is looked after, the food production part comes much more easily and will be more successful. And, further, when you come to hand over the land to the next generation, you can do so with pride.

Chapter One

Soils

This book is not a book on agriculture, or horticulture, but on estate management. Nevertheless a word about soil types may not be a bad thing, for everything we do on the land must be guided by the sort of land we have. Soil is derived in two different ways. It may derive from the rock beneath it, by the slow pulverization over millennia of the bedrock by water, frost, acids, living organisms, or the roots of plants. Or it may have been carried from afar and just dumped down where it is, by ice, wind or water. If your soil is of the former provenance, then it will have roughly the chemical quality of the rock beneath it. Thus if your soil is derived from a bedrock of chalk, then it will probably be calcareous in nature, for it is, in fact, simply chalk that has been pulverized by the factors I have listed above, mixed with the humus of dead plants and other organisms.

If, however, it is an erratic soil – having been brought from elsewhere – it need have no relationship to the rock below it at all. Such are the glacial 'tills' or 'boulder clays' which were carried from a distance in the Ice Age and dumped at random when the ice melted. Much of the soil of East Anglia and the English Midlands is like this. Geologists term these soils 'boulder clays' because they often have boulders in them. But often they neither have boulders nor are they clays. Glacial soils may vary from coarse gravel to heavy clay, and may be free of boulders or full of them. I have deposits of glacial-carried boulders on my farm in Pembrokeshire in Wales which hardly have any soil at all between the boulders. Other parts of the same farm are free of boulders altogether. East Anglia is, although much of it glacial, free from boulders. Much of it is heavy clay though. The vast fertile corn belt of the United States is made up of glacially transported soil.

It is very important to study the soil, either when you are contemplating buying a piece of land, or when you are preparing to improve a piece of land you have already got. Soil type is particularly important to consider when you are deciding what trees to plant. Trees are very fussy as to soil, and though much can be done to alter soil to suit the crop, it is always better to choose the right crop for the right soil.

Some soils have been carried to where they are by glacier, wind or water: others, such as soils on chalk or limestone, will probably have been derived from the underlying rock.

Clay soil

This is the heaviest soil, and it is indeed of a higher specific gravity than any others. This is because the particles that make it up are so small as to be quite invisible and therefore there are only the minutest air spaces in between. But clay soil is heavy in another way – it is heavy to work. To dig it with a spade can be back-breaking, and it can only be worked in dry weather, for to work it while it is wet is to cause it to 'puddle', or 'defloculate'.

This floculation and defloculation of clay is very important in its working. If clay soil is disturbed by cultivation when it is wet, the minute particles tend to come apart from one another and form an amorphous mass: exactly the consistency the potter wants. If clay soil is acid it tends to defloculate: fine for making pots, but useless for growing things. Defloculated clay is hardly permeable at all to water – therefore it takes an age to dry out. When it does dry out it become like lumps of brick, which no ordinary cultivation can break down. If the lumps are broken down by sheer mechanical force the soil becomes a sullen mass. When clay 'floculates', however, which it does when it is sufficiently alkaline, or when it is treated properly (i.e not worked when it is wet), the minute particles come together, by ionic action, into larger particles; water can move between the particles and so can air, and we have a fertile and kindly soil.

Most clay is alkaline but some is acid. Alkalinity or acidity are expressed by the pH scale, which is discussed at the end of this chapter. If this is below 6 in clay the soil certainly needs the addition of lime to it, and this will in time improve its texture (see Chapter 2). The other ways of improving its texture, whether it is acid or not, are: firstly, drainage, for badly drained soil seldom dries out and is therefore impossible to cultivate. It is also extremely bad for tree roots, for these cannot thrive in constant wet and therefore you get shallow-rooted trees which tend to blow over and do not thrive. Secondly, plough-ing or digging up in the autumn and leaving the ground turned up rough. This allows the frost to break down the lumps and both frost and air to 'sweeten' the soil. This is a complex process but is well understood by farmers and gardeners. The third, and most effective, is to incorporate much organic matter in the soil. You do not neces-sarily have to bury the organic matter: if you just leave it on top the earthworms will drag it down. *Any* organic matter will improve *any* soil. By organic matter is meant any matter that has formed part of a living thing. Thus hay, straw, dead leaves, grass, animal manure, seaweed (very valuable because of the minerals and trace elements it contains) – anything that has formed part of a living organism – will, if put on or in the land, rot down and become the magical stuff 'hu-mus' which will lighten and sweeten heavy clay. More on this subject in Chapter 2.

Clay soil is intrinsically fertile, and, properly drained and with add-ed humus (organic matter), will grow very fine crops of some things, if not others. Oak trees and apples thrive in it if it is well drained. So do roses. It must be noted that very few so-called 'clay soils' are composed solely of clay. A typical 'clay soil' may have sixty per cent clay in it and the rest silt and sand. A pure clay soil is stubborn stuff indeed, and of more use to the potter than to the farmer or horticul-turalist. The villainous 'adobe soils' of the western United States are clays which have undergone centuries of hot, dry weather. Adobe is usually looked upon as un-farmable, and yet the finest gardens I ever saw in my life were on such a soil: the transformation was achieved by the technique of 'deep bed' cultivation, plus unlimited application of an organic substance that is free for the taking from most 'beef lots' in western America: steer manure.

Loam

Happy is the person who comes into trusteeship of a loam soil! Loam is a mixture of clay, silt, sand and humus, and is probably the prod-uct, in Europe at least, of a forest soil that has been cultivated and manured for hundreds, or indeed thousands of years, by the farmer. It tends to be deep, well drained, easy to cultivate (even when rea-sonably damp, unlike clay), easy for roots to penetrate, and full of nutrients. Loams can need draining, they can be too acid and therefore need liming, but otherwise the husbandman is unlikely to have many problems with them and nearly everything he wishes to cultivate will flourish on them.

Calcareous soil

This is soil on chalk or limestone rock from which the soil has been formed. Such soil is invariably well drained and normally, as one would expect, does not need liming – *being* lime. Surprisingly though a few soils on limestone do need liming; presumably the available calcium in them has been leached out or locked up. Calcareous soils are easy to work (they have no lay component), healthy for stock, good for certain crops (high quality malting barley grows on them) and the fine springy healthful grass turf that grows on the chalk downs is famous.

A problem in growing certain trees on limestone or chalk (particularly chalk) is that the trees tend to take up too much calcium, their leaves go yellow and they die. Most conifers do badly, if at all, on chalk soils. The only conifers that will grow on very calcareous soils are: larch (because the leaves fall every autumn thus ridding the tree of its calcium load), Western Red and Atlas Cedars, Corsican Pine and Lawson Cyprus. The tree to plant on chalk or limestone *par excellence* is of course the beech. This revels in a calcareous soil and should always form the bulk of planting in such areas.

Peat soil

This is composed of nothing but organic matter. Seeing that organic matter is so desireable in all other soil types, and can be seen to do nothing but good, it is surprising that soil composed of organic matter is barren.

But the reason why peat soil was formed in the first place was that the land was so wet and ill-drained that vegetable matter could not rot, but fermented to form what we call peat. If such peat beds are covered by the encroaching sea, and then subjected to pressure from sediments that are deposited on top of them, they turn into coal, and in this manner our coal measures were formed.

In wet climates peat, particularly if it is deep, can be very intractable and good for very little. It will grow potatoes (which is why the people in the West of Ireland grow such quantities of them) and celery, but very little else. Deep wetland peat can be planted with trees, mainly conifers, also alder and ash, provided the land can be drained effectively and phosphates added, in which it is deficient.

The peat soils of the Fens in the East of England are another kettle of fish altogether. Better soil than this can be found nowhere. These peats have silt, from old lakes and the sea, added to them, they are naturally free draining, and produce some of the finest crops in the world. They are a wasting asset though – being organic, they are actually used up by the crops they produce – and in parts of the Fens the peat, once many yards deep, has now gone entirely, leaving the sullen clay below. The wind, too, in this dry eastern climate, carries hundreds of tons of peat dust away every spring and early summer, often with the seeds of the crop in it. So anyone coming into possession of the precious asset of dry peatland should nurture it by planting trees on it, hedges, putting it down to grass from time to time, and organic manuring.

Sandy soil

This can vary from pure dune sand to very impure sand, such as the greensands of southern England. The Breckland country of west Norfolk and Suffolk and the sandling country of the Suffolk coast are typical sandy soils. They are invariably free draining – that is if the water table is low enough the soil itself will dry out very quickly – they have the advantage of being very *early* soils (they warm up quickly in the spring and stay warm in the summer), they suffer badly from drought unless they can be irrigated, they are very easy to cultivate and can be ploughed or dug in the wettest weather, they tend to be acid and need lime. They tend to be lacking in plant nutrients and grow poor crops unless well manured. They are 'hungry' soils: if you apply organic manure to them they eat it up very quickly – it soon goes. They can be improved though: plenty of organic manure (they cannot have too much), green manuring (growing leguminous crops, such as clovers and lucerne that do well on them), liming if necessary, and heavy stocking with animals (the 'golden hoof' of sheep folded on turnips transformed the poor sands of North Norfolk in the early part of the nineteenth century, and pigs run on sandy land do well and 'do' the soil); I would recommend light or sandy soils to the small estate owner.

Gravel Soil

Old Cobbett, in his *Rural Rides* (the record of his rides round the country in the early nineteenth century), was constantly fulminating against the 'spewy gravels of East Surrey': fit for nothing but rhododendrons, birch trees and beggarly pines and, as Cobbett always used to point out: 'the villas of stock jobbers.' But even gravel soils can be improved enormously by the addition of plenty of organic manure, and an excellent idea is to fold pigs over them.

Podsol

This is the term given to soil found under heathland, which is pretty poor stuff to start off with. This is why it has been left under heather, gorse, bracken or other plants of the heathland. On digging down into it we see that it has become layered. At the top will be a narrow brown layer which contains some organic material, beneath this a pale zone from which all the nutrients have been leached out by water, and below this, typically, a hard reddish 'pan', which is a narrow layer into which all the soluble elements from above have been deposited – notably oxide of iron.

To grow anything worthwhile in podsol (except cranberries) we must sub-soil (i.e. drag vertical steel blades through the soil to some depths) deep enough to break up this impervious pan, and plough very deeply to mix the various layers of the soil, lime if necessary, and then incorporate plenty of organic manure. Perhaps a crop of such trees as silver birch should be taken from it first so that their roots can bring up nutrients from the sub-soil and their leaves add organic matter to the top.

Such are the soil types we are likely to be blessed with (some unhappy landowners may say cursed) but it is my contention that practically any soil in the world can be made productive and fruitful, provided enough knowledge, love and care are brought to bear on it. It is Man's destiny and privilege to bring every kind of soil, good or bad, up to its highest state of biological productivity.

As for the matter of pH, or the acidity-alkalinity status of soils, this can be tested very easily, by anybody at all, with a simple kit bought from a garden store or chemist's. Simple throw a little soil into a test tube, pour in a reagent from a bottle, and note what colour it goes. The colour can be checked against a colour chart, which gives you your pH.

The following is a table of possible soils classified as to their pH.

pH	Soil condition	Plants suited to it
3.5 – 4.0	Extremely acid. Some forest soil only.	None.
4.0 – 4.5	Wet forest soil or wet peat.	None.
4.5 – 5.0	Acid. West heathland, etc.	Cranberries, blueberries, rhododendrons.
5.0 – 5.5	Acid but not impossible.	Potatoes, tomatoes, strawberries.
5.5 – 6.0	Slightly acid.	Most crops will grow but some not very well.
6.0 – 6.5	Neutral.	Most crops and trees will grow well.
6.5 – 7.5	Neutral to alkaline.	Most crops but not solanaceous family (potato and tomato family) or rhododendrons.
7.5 – 8.0	Much too alkaline. Found only in some desert areas such as western United States.	None.

Chapter Two

Improvement of Land

In temperate climates this very often just means drainage. In dry climates it means irrigation.

Drainage

Few plants that are useful to man will grow in waterlogged land. There are exceptions to this: the Swamp Cyprus (*Taxodium distichum*) will grow actually *in* water (although it has to be started off on a temporary mound just above it) as it has special tubes to take air down to its roots. It is a beautiful tree and yields good timber. More should be planted. Rice (called 'paddy' right through what was British India, the word rice meaning the hulled grain) grows in water too, although it didn't grow successfully when I sowed some in Pembrokeshire. Watercress of course we all know, and water chestnuts grow in slightly warmer climates than the British one.

But, after naming these exceptions, we get back to the truth of the matter: nearly everything you want to grow, or see growing, will do better on well drained land than on wet. And here we have an anomaly. Grass growing on waterlogged ground commonly suffers more from *drought* than that grown on well drained land. The reason is that on waterlogged ground the roots of the grasses cannot go down far and therefore the grasses have small and weak root systems. During a drought the water table sinks in the wet ground, and the shallow-rooted grasses cannot get enough moisture from the now dry earth. Whereas grasses growing on well drained land push their roots deep down into the soil, develop a vigorous and extensive root system, and so can extract what water there is in the earth from a wide area.

Wet land furthermore is sour (acid) and infertile; vegetable matter that falls on it will not rot and thus release its nutrients for other plant life. So you get peat; which is made of layer upon layer of dead

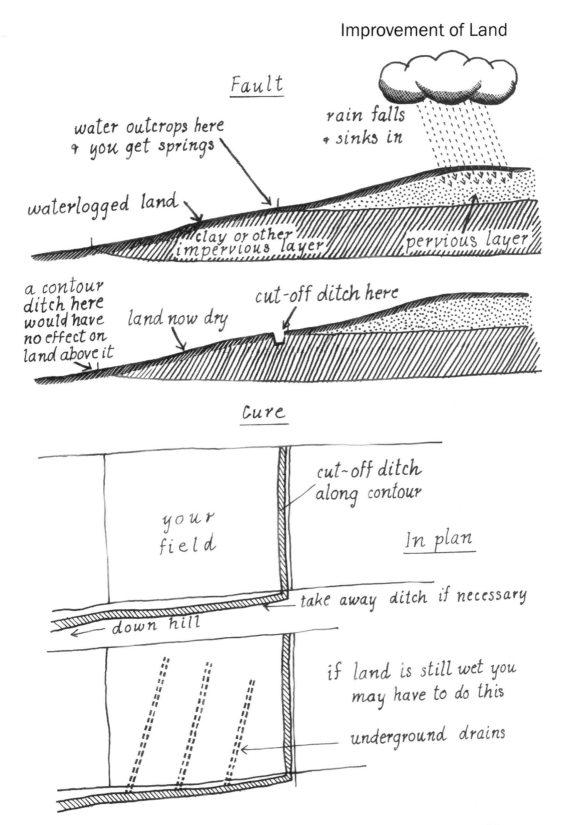

Fault

rain falls
& sinks in

water outcrops here
& you get springs

waterlogged land

clay or other
impervious layer

pervious layer

a contour
ditch here
would have
no effect on
land above it

land now dry

cut-off ditch here

Cure

your
field

cut-off ditch
along contour

In plan

take away ditch if necessary

down hill

if land is still wet you
may have to do this

underground drains

vegetable matter which has not been allowed to rot by the anaerobic conditions of wet land. About the only crops such land in temperate climates will grow are celery and potatoes, and the only tree is the Sitka Spruce – and then only if the land is ridged first and the crop grown on top of the drier ridges.

Other disadvantages of wet land are: grassland 'poaches' much more under the feet of cattle, tractor tyres, and so on (poaching – a polite modern way of saying 'pochin' which is an onomatopoeic word derived from the pludging of an animal's hooves into wet mud and means damage done to the surface of land by trampling animals when the land is wet). You can graze land later in the autumn and earlier in the spring if it is well drained. Wet land is late land. So much of the sun's heat is used just to dry it out that the sun does not warm the soil in the spring and seedlings suffer from this. The evaporation of water from soil uses up heat by latent heat of evaporation. Wet land cannot be ploughed or dug until much later in the season than dry. And, in grassland, wet land will contain less nutritious flora than dry and furthermore, is apt to harbour the horrid little snail that is a vector for liver fluke, which may attack sheep, cattle, and even you.

So there is every reason for draining wet land. And all land, so far as I know, can be drained. Even land which is below the sea, as in Dutch *polders*, can be drained. The water is led to the lowest point – a 'sump' – and thence pumped up into embanked rivers which carry it to the sea. But some land is very expensive to drain and sometimes not worth draining. Also, surely we have a duty to leave some wetland for the creatures that live there.

Rain falls on the surface of the earth and, if the earth is bare of vegetation, as it shouldn't be, some of it runs off and carries with it some of the soil and this is known as erosion. It is a thing to be prevented. If the soil is covered with vegetation, all the water soaks into it and continues to penetrate downwards through the pervious soil until it comes to an impervious layer. It then builds up, and tries to move laterally, if it can, through the pervious layers. If the land is sloping and the layers of soil and rock are flat the chances are that the latter will 'outcrop'. That means they will end exposed on the hillside. When an impervious layer outcrops, above it the *water* will outcrop

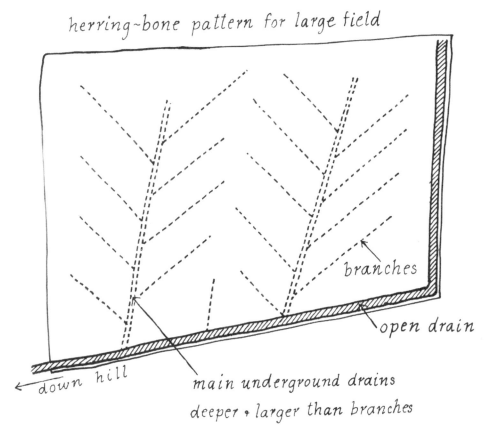

herring-bone pattern for large field

branches

open drain

← down hill

main underground drains

deeper + larger than branches

and a line of springs results. My farmhouse in Wales is built on such an outcrop, and, until I drained it, water used to bubble up through the slates in the kitchen floor. The water will then trickle down the surface of the slope, over the impervious sub-soil, and you get a wet field.

It is no good digging a ditch along the contour at the *bottom* of this wet field. The water in the field doesn't even know that the ditch is there. It just slowly keeps percolating downwards and – true – in the end it will find its way into the ditch, but by then it will have done its work of giving you a wet field. The only person who will benefit is your neighbour below the ditch. You will have drained his land, not your own.

It is little good, either, digging ditches down the slope. If you do this you only drain the land within a few feet each side of the ditch. It *may* be necessary, though (in fact it probably will be), to dig at least one down-the-slope ditch simply to take the water away from the horizontal, or contour, ditch which is actually going to do your draining for you.

The way to drain your field is to dig a contour ditch along the *top* of the field. Uninformed people are apt to say: 'What is the good of digging a ditch along the contour at the top of the field – the water in the soil below it – in the field – does not even know the ditch is there!' What they don't realize is that you drain the field by preventing water from getting into it – not by removing the water which is already there. I was responsible for carrying out hundreds of land-draining schemes in East Suffolk just after the war – and it took me a little time to understand this principle.

The contour ditch along the top of the field you wish to drain is called the 'cut-off ditch'. The one at right angles to this that carries the water away down the slope is called the 'carry-away ditch'. If there happens to be a stream running down the slope in the right place you won't need one of the latter – you merely let your cut-off ditch discharge into the stream.

Rain will still fall on to your field below the cut-off ditch. Probably this will not be enough to waterlog the field. But what you must remember is that there may be more outcrops of water further down the field, which will have escaped your cut-off ditch by going underneath it. You will get springs again, and wet patches. What you need here is another horizontal cut-off ditch, parallel to the first one.

But you can't cut up your field with innumerable cut-off ditches. So what you do is to lay an underground drain there. Now it is all right for an open ditch to be exactly horizontal – to follow the contour exactly. Provided the water can get out of one end of the ditch, the ditch will always be empty, which is the way you want it. (I've heard townspeople say 'This ditch is not working – there is no water in it!' The fact that it *is* working accounts for there being no water in it.) But with an underground drain you want some fall, or slope, to keep the small pipe scoured out and clear of silting. Thus you site your underground drain at an angle to the contour of the field, so that it runs at

To drain a wet _level_ field

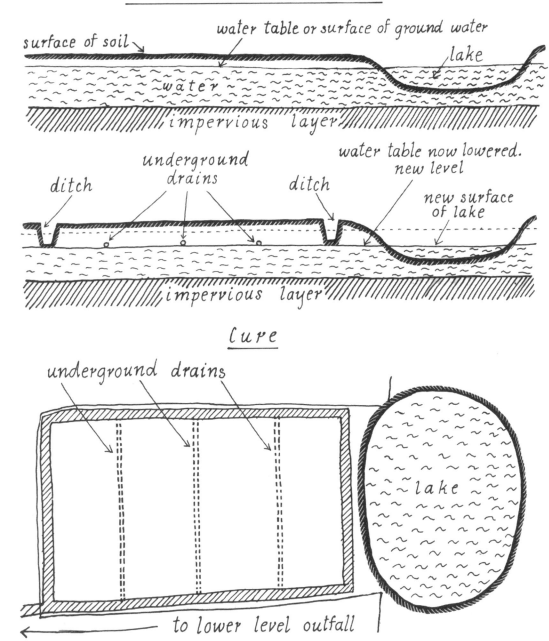

Cure

Inclusion of lake in the illustration is to show the principle of lowering water table - it is essential for drainage!

an even angle slightly downhill. It must then, eventually, discharge into your carry-away ditch – or into a stream.

Now if the land is perfectly *flat*, and there is an impervious layer underneath the pervious soil and subsoil, you will get a stationary water table at some depth beneath the surface of the soil, or, in bad cases, level with it, in which case you have a swamp. If the water table (the surface of the standing water) is *above* the surface of the soil, you have a lake.

To drain such land (yes – you can even drain a lake) you have to *lower* the water table. It is not a matter of a cut-off drain to prevent water from coming into the field from above, but simply of drains that have their bottoms at a lower level than that of the water table. The water then percolates through the soil into them and is carried away. Of course it's got to *be* carried away: it's no good just digging ditches that don't lead out anywhere. Such ditches will always be full of water, the water table will remain just as high and your field will still be a swamp.

I describe these first principles of land drainage because without a grasp of them people often do a lot of work and spend a lot of money and still fail to drain their land. The illustrations, I hope, will make the matter plainer than my words can.

People will tell you that you need 'an expert' to drain land. What you need in fact is OMCS: Old Mother Common Sense. There is no mystery in it at all. Experience helps, though, and in difficult cases the advice of an experienced neighbour can be of great help. Of course if it's grants you're after (like the old farmer who woke up from a deep sleep during the church service when the minster said: 'Grant we beseech thee…' and said to his wife: 'What's that about a grant?') then you have to get the government drainage officer in and do what he says. But on a small scale, and with small areas of land, you will probably not be eligible for a grant anyway and it is far better to do it yourself.

The first thing to do is to dig, with a spade, or else with an earth auger if you have one, a few test holes. Go down for at least three feet – four is not too much – and you will thus get some information about the structure of your soil and sub-soil. If the land needs draining you will soon come to water, and the water will not go away just because you have dug a hole down to it. It will just stand in the hole and you will then know how high the water table is at that particular time of the year and in that particular place. Of course it is likely to be higher in the winter than it is in a dry summer. If it is not more than two and a half feet below the surface of your land, it is too high, for plant roots need at least that depth of unwaterlogged soil. Personally I like to see the water table as low as four feet below the surface, but three is acceptable. Water travels upwards through otherwise dry soil by 'capillary attraction'. This is the force that causes water to move upwards through minute apertures: such as the minute apertures between grains of soil. Thus, even if the ground water is quite low, enough of it will travel upwards to supply the roots of your plants.

Your test holes will show you the nature of your sub-soil and give an indication of how deep to place your drains. For example, if you go through three feet of soil and then come to solid clay, it would be better to place any pipe drains (underground drains) so that they are lying on the surface of the clay – not deeper. The open ditch into which they debouch can well be a foot or even eighteen inches deeper than this – for it must have a fall from the collars (outlets) of the drains. And, remember, the underground drains themselves must have a steady fall all their lengths. This fall can be as small as 1 in 100, but it must be continuous: a 'sump', or low place, in the drain is bound to lead to silting up. Even in dead flat land it is possible to arrange for a fall – the drain starts, at its furthest from the ditch, shallow and enters the ditch at a deeper level. No drain should ever be shallower than two and a half feet: if it is, plant roots may block it up and deep cultivations disturb it. Four foot deep, at its lower point, is not too deep. Incidentally, underground drains should not be too near trees: twenty feet is about the minimum. Roots will enter the pipes and block them. Ash trees in particular send their roots spectacular distances through the soil. If it is necessary to put them near trees, use plastic pipes with no holes in them for that section.

In peat soil it is far better to put your drains right down on the solid ground (probably sand, gravel or clay) beneath the peat. If you lay them higher up they will twist and bend as the peat settles in some

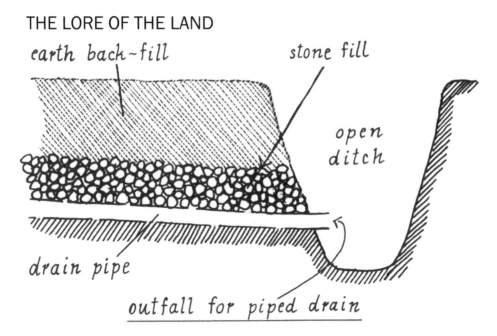

places and not in others. If the peat is too deep for this, open ditches are the best way to drain it. The intervals between drains vary according to soil: from fifteen feet apart in heavy clay to forty in sand.

Springs should be sought out and dealt with. Springs will appear in the most unexpected places; they are not always signalled by visible water, but often merely by wet patches on the surface of the ground beneath them. When springs are the result of an outcropping of water caused by a permeable layer on top of an impermeable one, they are apt to occur in a line along a contour. These are best dealt with by an open ditch (the 'cut-off ditch' we have already described). But single springs are sometimes the result of water coming up from under an impermeable layer (see illustration). Such water is often under pressure, and gets forced to the surface up fissures in the impermeable layer. This is in reality 'artesian' water – water pushed to the surface by the weight of the water behind it and up-slope from it. It accounts for there being springs right at the tops of hills in some cases. Where this occurs you can be sure that there are higher hills nearby, and a connection by permeable layer underneath impermeable between the higher hills and your mysterious hill-top spring.

To mitigate the baleful effect of a spring you must tap it. Dig a carry-away ditch or lay an underground drain uphill from an existing drain, ditch or stream to the spring. This must of course have a steady fall. Dig then a sump, or well, at the site of the spring – and

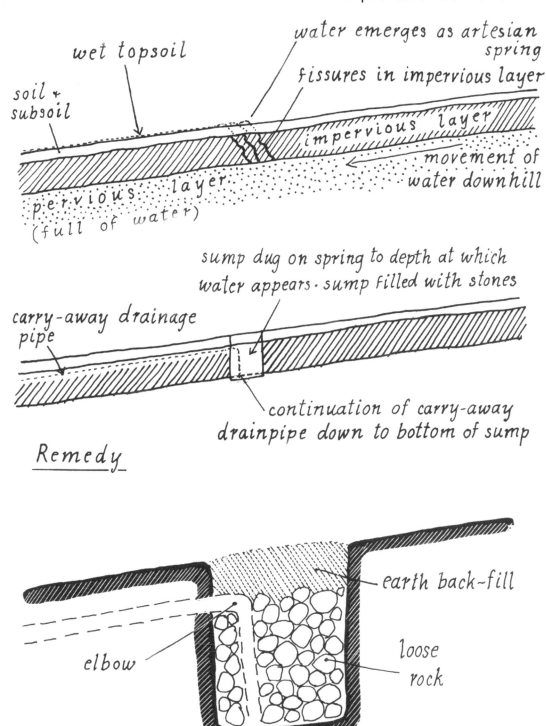

wet topsoil

water emerges as artesian spring

fissures in impervious layer

soil + subsoil

impervious layer

pervious layer (full of water)

movement of water downhill

sump dug on spring to depth at which water appears. sump filled with stones

carry-away drainage pipe

continuation of carry-away drainpipe down to bottom of sump

Remedy

earth back-fill

elbow

loose rock

keep digging down until you reach strongly running water. Place an elbow joint on the drain pipe, and fit a vertical piece of pipe going down to near the bottom of the well you have dug. Fill the hole with stones and then top up with some of the earth you have dug out. In many cases you will find, in practice, that you do not need the elbow and piece of vertical pipe: the spring will be shallow enough for you to tap it without such a contraption. Sometimes a large wet patch in a field can be drained completely by simply tapping this one spring.

Now to discuss the various types and forms of drains that you might lay.

The **open ditch** is just what it says it is, and it has its advantages and disadvantages. An advantage is that if it gets blocked up you can see it is blocked up and easily clear it. It is extremely efficient at carrying water away. You know just where you are with it. Disadvantages are that it takes up good land, it has to be fenced to keep stock out of it (it is amazing how quickly cattle clambering down into a ditch – and out again – will break down its sides and pigs will quickly fill it in completely). It requires almost annual maintenance to keep it working. Every year the vegetation that grows in it must be 'flashed out' – that is cut away – and every few years the silt must be cleaned out. If you do this with a machine it costs; if with a shovel it tires.

Open ditches can be dug by man or machine. Prisoners-of-war dug hundreds of miles of them during and after the last war, and Irish contractors, generally working in pairs, could dig them so quickly that, at piece-work rates, they were earning four times the minimum agricultural wage. Nowadays it is generally considered that the work is too arduous to do by hand (in any case too expensive) and it is done by machine: generally the ubiquitous JCB. The things to remember when digging them by any method are to avoid 'sumps' – in other words to have the bottom as level as possible; and to *batter* the sides – have them sloping outwards – and this depends on the type of ground. Ditches dug in clay do not need such a batter as ones dug in sand. Good OMCS should tell you what sort of batter to give – you can soon feel if it is enough to prevent the sides falling in again.

An interesting thing here is that whoever owns the ditch also owns the hedge, for good or for evil. And it is not the hedge that is the

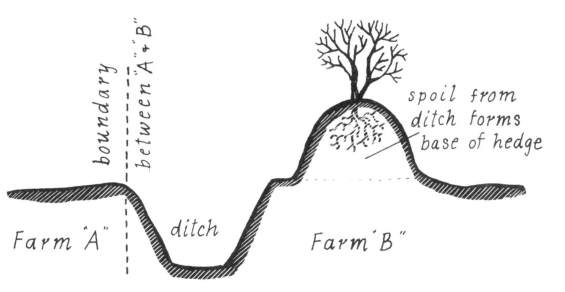

boundary – but the lip of the ditch further from the hedge! This is not what one would expect but is made necessary by the fact that he who maintains the ditch needs the space of the hedge to fling the 'spoil' (removed earth) out onto and that is inevitably the ground at the base of the hedge. When you first dig a ditch down your border with a neighbour you cannot fling the spoil onto his land (he wouldn't like it) and therefore you throw it back onto your own. And on the top of the bank thus formed you plant a hedge. If you don't, one grows.

Now **underground drains** can be of many types, as we shall discuss in a minute. They have the advantages that they don't take up good land (you plough or dig over them), they don't have to be maintained, often for many decades, and they don't have to be fenced. Disadvantages are that you can't see what is happening to them, and if they *do* get silted up, or blocked by roots, you have a hell of a job digging them right up and laying them again.

The Romans used **brush drains** (also called 'bush' drains) and so sometimes do we. You just dig a trench, lay brushwood in the bottom of it and cover this with earth. The brushwood allows the water to percolate through, and when it rots the earth may still stay open for many years and allow water through. I have used short lengths of brushwood drains with very good results, and brushwood has the advantage that it is free.

31

Cross-sections of drains.

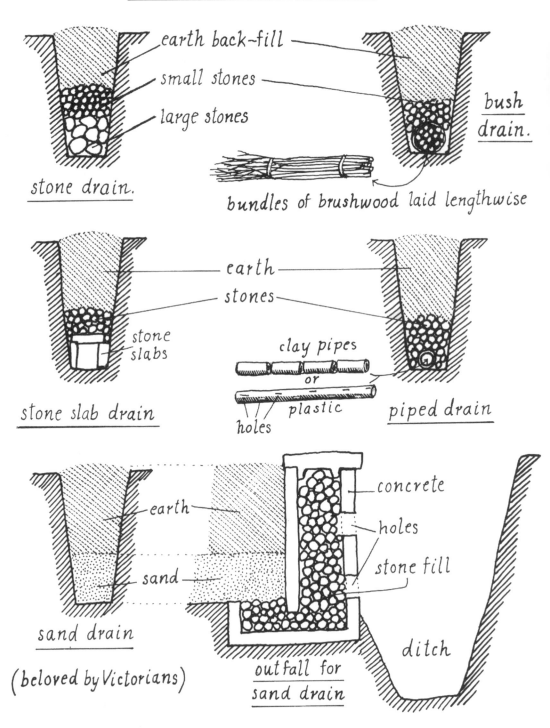

earth back-fill

small stones

large stones

bush drain.

stone drain.

bundles of brushwood laid lengthwise

earth

stones

stone slabs

stone slab drain

clay pipes
or
plastic

holes

piped drain

earth

sand

sand drain

(beloved by Victorians)

concrete

holes

stone fill

outfall for sand drain

ditch

Stone drains are not impossible. Just dig the trench, chuck large stones in, small stones on top of them, then backfill with earth. They will, after many years, get silted up. In Wales, when we dig down in wet places, we sometimes uncover another kind of stone drain – the **stone slab drain**. This is just a line of flat stones set on edge on each side of the old trench covered with a roof of more flat stones. These are extremely effective and some are still working after a hundred years. It is a well recommended method on small areas of land, when the work is done by the owner and therefore is done with love and care.

With the coming of the agricultural revolution in the early nineteenth century landowners came out with several kinds of tile drains. 'Tile' simply meant fired earthenware. After trying tiles of different sections they finally came up with round tiles, three inches in internal diameter for side branches and four inches for the mains, each tile about ten inches long. The sections are simply laid end to end and there is quite enough space for the water to get into them at the places where they join The tiles *must* be covered with stone fill – broken stone about one and a half to two inches diameter is best. In days of yore a groove just the diameter of the pipe was scooped out at the bottom of the trench: this is no longer done as it inhibits the ingress of water into the pipe.

Now **plastic pipes** have practically taken the place of tiles. The pipes come in long sections, which fit together, and have slits in them to let the water in. they are extremely light to carry and easy to lay. They bridge uneven places in the bottom of the trench better than tiles. How long they last is anybody's guess – they haven't been going long enough for anybody to know. They seem alright. But I remember, in 1947, opening a drain in heavy land in Suffolk (the open ditch into which it debouched was silted up) and water immediately began to gush out of it. There was a date on the cast-iron collar through which it ended at the ditch and the date was 1849.

A hundred years ago **sand drains** were very popular. I have never come across any but it seems to me that they might be cheap and effective. The water would not gush out of them so quickly as it does through pipes but this might not be a bad thing 'Softly, softly' is a good motto in land drainage, as in other things. The sand drains had a rather complicated egress into the ditch, which is best shown in the illustration. This was the only way of holding the sand in. This is the only form of drain of which I have not had personal experience, but it might be well worth trying – particularly if you have a ready and cheap supply of sand available.

Mole drains are a cheap and easy way of draining – if you have the right soil. Nowadays this is done by a heavy tractor pulling a cylinder of steel through the earth held at the bottom of a steel plate. The steel plate cuts a slot through the earth which subsequently gets closed up; the cylinder cuts a hole about three or four inches in diameter which stays open. The hole has to have an even fall to the ditch and debouch into it. In suitable soil (with a high clay content) moles will stay open for twenty years – eight or ten is more likely. But they are cheap to do. Often they are used in conjunction with pipe drains.

There is one other drainage technique to consider and that is **subsoiling.** One has often stood in a horrible wet field and then walked to the edge of the ditch to see dry drain outlets. What is happening is that there is a hard impervious 'pan' beneath the topsoil – possibly caused by ploughs always pressing along at the same depth. The surface water just cannot get down to the drains. What is needed here is something to break up the pan. It can be done by tractor pulling a sub-soiler – an instrument with deep blades cutting into the soil. Or you can do it yourself by deep-digging with a spade.

If you only have a small piece of land, do not be alarmed at all the above technicalities. Quite likely your land does not need draining at all: much land doesn't. Or if it does, maybe a simple cut-off ditch or drain along the top of it will do it, or maybe just the tapping of one spring. But if it does need draining, drain it – because no other action will make so much difference to the success of your growing operations, nor the health of yourself and your stock.

Where a road or path goes across a ditch you either have to have a footbridge or a 'culvert'. The latter is simply made by laying a concrete pipe of sufficient size to carry storm water right down at the level of the bottom of the ditch, with the entry end of the pipe a few inches below the bottom of the ditch and the outlet end a few inches above it; there should be at least eighteen inches of earth on top of

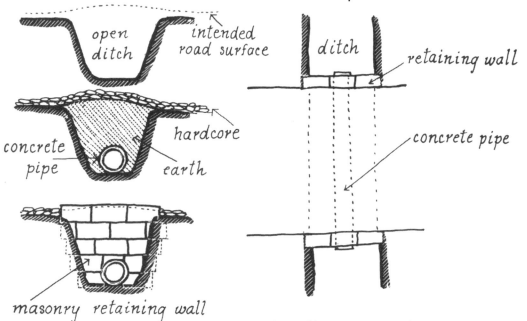

open ditch

intended road surface

hardcore

concrete pipe

earth

masonry retaining wall

ditch

retaining wall

concrete pipe

constructing culvert under road.

King post bridge

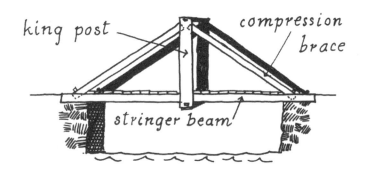

king post

compression brace

stringer beam

for longer bridges –
2 king posts make a Queen post truss.

the pipe and this earth must be retained by the building of a concrete, stone or brick retaining wall at each end of the culvert. These walls must be keyed into the earth at each side of the ditch. Hardcore or other hard surface should be laid on the roadway on top.

A couple of long railway sleepers make a good footbridge over a ditch. For wider streams a king post bridge is more appropriate, and for even wider ones (say twenty feet) a queen post will be stronger. The illustrations show these constructions.

Soil treatment

Analyse your soil using a test kit available from garden centres. If you have a gross deficiency of lime, phosphorus, nitrogen or potash, remedy by applying one of the dressings below:

Nitrogen – for leaf production
Phosphorous - for root and fruit production
Potash – for flower production

Lime. A normal dressing of lime would be 1 ton to the acre, or about ½lb to 10 square feet. If the land is very acid you might put on as much as 3 tons to the acre (for a pH of 5 or under) or 1½lb per 10 square feet.

Farmyard Manure. Twenty tons of this to the acre would be a suitable dressing (if you can get it!) which works out at roughly 1,000lb to 1,000 square feet, or 100lb to 100 square feet, or 1lb to a square foot. Poultry or rabbit manure could go on at about half this rate.

Phosphorus. A pound of ground rock phosphate to 10 square feet should correct any normal phosphate deficiency, and if, subsequently, plenty of organic manure of some sort is added to the soil it should be many years before phosphate deficiency will rear its ugly head again. Bone meal, dried blood, fish meal and activated sewage sludge are also good sources of phosphates. *Basic Slag*, a by-product of the steel industry, is a good source of phosphate for grassland. Half a ton to the acre is a reasonable dose – but if analysis shows gross phosphate deficiency you could cheerfully double this, as a once-only application, best applied in the autumn.

Blood meal. Or dried blood, is very high in nitrogen (up to 15%) and should either be used as a boost for plants in the early growing season or, better in my opinion, as a compost activator. Keep a bag near the compost heap and just add a sprinkling to each five or six inches of vegetable material as you add it. This will speed up the compost-making process exceedingly and also turn out a very fine, nitrogen-rich compost. The 3% phosphorus it contains is a bonus too.

Bone meal. Has a mere 2 to 4% nitrogen but a very high 20 to 25% phosphoric acid, and is therefore generally applied for its phosphorus alone. If you can get it it is excellent as a source of phosphorus. It may be helpful to include the following table:

100lb per acre equals 2½ lb per 1,000 square feet or ½ oz
per square yard.
1 ton an acre equals 50lb per 1,000 square feet or ½ lb per square
yard.
Most bagged fertilizers weigh about 1lb to a pint.

Compost. Should be the mainstay of all land improvement programmes. It can be put on the soil at any time, either laid on top or else dug or rotovated in. Two inches of compost spread on all soil once a year will keep the soil in perfect condition, once any gross deficiencies have been remedied, and if it is possible to maintain that rate of application it should never be necessary to apply any mineral fertilizers again. And there is just no such thing as anybody applying too much compost.

Sewage sludge and *Municipal composts.* These are often available for very cheap prices and, although they are enormously variable in content, can be very good value. *Activated sludge*, which has had air pumped through it to encourage aerobic bacterial activity, can contain 5% nitrogen and from 3 to 5% phosphorus. Municipal compost varies enormously, and it would be useless to try to give any analysis. It should be used in much the same manner as garden compost.

A caveat about all municipal sewage material is that it *can* contain dangerous amounts of toxic chemicals. Lead and cadmium are two metals that are sometimes present in damaging quantities. The vendors of the sludge or compost should declare the presence of any such materials. One application of material containing such chemicals is most unlikely to do any harm but repeated applications could prove very harmful.

The general rules about *when* to apply fertilizers are that it is best to put on phosphatic or potassic fertilizers in the autumn before planting a crop, or in the winter, while quick-acting nitrogenous manures should be put on just before the crop is planted or even during its growth. Lime can be added at any time of the year when it is convenient. As a general rule it is best not to lime heavily the same year as a heavy application of an organic manure such as farmyard manure is put on.

Chapter Three

Grassland

Of all the crops that mankind husbands, grass is the most wide-spread and most important. And by 'grass' here I am not including the various corn crops that belong to the grass family – wheat, barley, oats, maize, rye, and so on – but I am including plants which are not even remotely related to grass – clovers, lucerne and also certain deep rooting herbs. Grass never grows, in nature, completely alone, and it should not do so in mankind's husbandry systems either: except when, as occasionally it must be, grass of one species is grown for seed.

The small landowner is likely to use grass for the following purposes: lawn, feeding grazing animals, making hay to feed animals, improving arable land.

The last use is one of the very important employments of grass. Dr William Davies, Director of the Grassland Research Station of Hurley, wrote in the *Journal of the Soil Association* that:

> The ploughing in of a grass sward is something more than merely one of the ways of incorporating organic matter with the soil. Grass roots have a peculiar power of causing the aggregation of soil particles into crumbs, and a good crumb structure, so long as it persists, results in the easy production of a good mellow tilth and in maintaining a good air-and-water relationship. The ley, in short, has two distinct functions – to produce animal feed and to improve soil condition.

Every farmer knows that there is no better way of reviving exhausted land than by growing a grass 'ley' on it. A 'ley' means a plant of grass (and clover) laid down for a number of years and then ploughed up again. You can have a one-year-ley, a two-year-ley, and so on. Six year leys are used in some forms of organic rotations. Anything much longer than that and you may as well be done with it and call it a 'permanent pasture', but there is a tendency nowadays, and a good one, to plough grassland up and re-seed it every ten years or so.

A ley and a permanent pasture are two quite different things. A ley can be very productive, very nutritious, and very good for the soil when it is ploughed in again. Permanent pasture, *at its best*, is the best feeding for grazing animals in the world. At its worst (all too common), it is rubbish. Good permanent pasture is like climax forest: it is climax vegetation. It would, if it were allowed to, turn into forest, but it is not allowed to because of grazing animals. Grass and clover can stand up to heavy grazing: baby trees cannot. But it is only the most exceptional permanent grassland that would not benefit from being ploughed up and re-seeded.

It may increase one's understanding to realize that grass belongs to the great division of the plant kingdom called 'monocotyledon'. In the other division – the bicotyledons – the leaves grow from their ends and edges. Therefore every time an animal nibbles a leaf, the growing area of that leaf is destroyed. The leaf cannot repair itself. Grass, however, belonging to the other great natural division, does not grow out from the ends of its narrow leaves, but pushes the leaves out from the base. The growing point of a grass (or any other 'monocot') leaf is at its base – not its tip. Therefore animals may nibble away as much as they like – the plant simply extrudes more leaves from the un-nibbled bases. Thus 'monocots' stand up to grazing much better than 'bicots'.

Clovers, though, are bicots. Their growing points are outwards. When a clover plant is nipped off, its growing points are nipped off too. It is only because it has great reserves of nourishment in its roots – *and* the capacity to manufacture its own nitrogen – that it manages to survive hard grazing. Clover also manages to cling very closely to the soil where it is difficult for grazing animals to get at it. Or lawn mowers for that matter.

Now good pasture, or ley, should be a concerto played between clovers and grasses. The two are complementary. The clovers (being members of the family *leguminosae*) have bacteria in nodules on their roots that have the power of taking nitrogen from the air and combining this with oxygen to form compounds that more complex plants can make use of. Thus the more clover you have in a field, the more nitrogen that will be 'fixed' and the more fertile, at any rate in terms of nitrogen, the field will be. Grass, on the other hand, does *not* fix nitrogen, but uses a lot of it. But grass provides a great bulk of very nutritious fodder for grazing animals. It is hardy and drought-resistant. It stands up during the winter – when all clovers jut die back and cannot be seen. It stands up to hard tramping.

So a judicious mixture of grasses and clovers is what you want. All grazing animals thrive on such a mixture, and it makes the best of hay. I once bought a load of hay which was all Italian rye grass, from a field which had been heavily laced with nitrogenous fertilizer. There was not a leaf of clover in it. The stuff was quite inedible, and in the end I had to use it for bedding.

Now if you add fixed nitrogen (nitrogenous fertilizer) to your land you will encourage your grass but suppress your clover. You will, if you add enough N (the symbol for nitrogen) without phosphates completely destroy your clover. You will get a greater bulk of grass by doing it – but remember, you will be paying dearly for this bulk. For you will have not one unit of free nitrogen because you won't have any clover. As compounds containing N soar ever higher in price, this becomes a less and less sensible thing to do. Surely it is better to be satisfied with a smaller bulk of fodder but not have to pay for it? And, further, the quality of the fodder will be higher if it is grown naturally without high nitrogen inputs: this has been shown experimentally time and again. The first two hundredweight of nitrogenous fertilizer you apply will do you no good whatever: they will merely supply the N which *would* have been supplied free by the bacteria in the root nodules of the clover. Any dose in excess of that will begin to increase yield – but at what a cost! Personally I would not dream of putting an ounce of nitrogenous fertilizer on any grassland. This does not mean that I do not like 'nitrogen'. I do like 'nitrogen', but I like it free and natural.

Phosphates, however, are a different thing. The clovers need plenty of the element phosphorus, and if you apply phosphates to your grassland you will encourage the clovers at the expense of the grasses. In the end the grasses, too, will benefit, because they, being nitrogen-

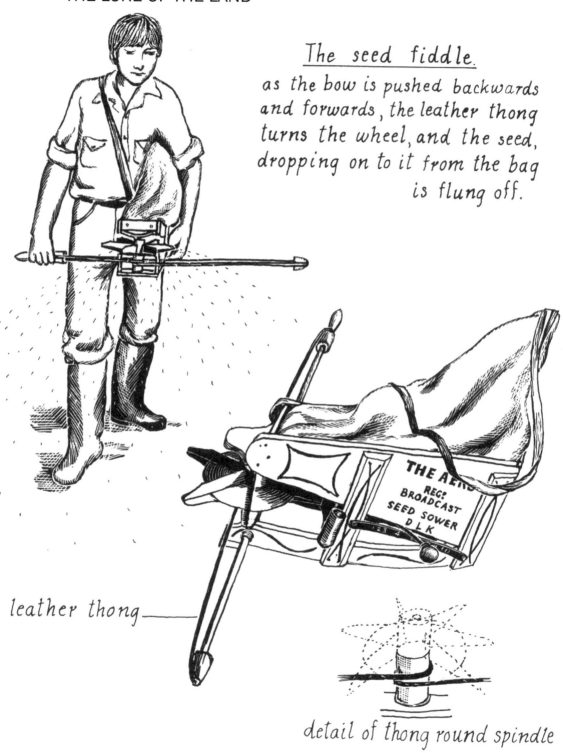

The seed fiddle.

as the bow is pushed backwards and forwards, the leather thong turns the wheel, and the seed, dropping on to it from the bag is flung off.

THE AER...
REG:
BROADCAST
SEED SOWER
D L K

leather thong

detail of thong round spindle

lovers, will grow vigorous from the N that the clovers supply. Lime, too, is important. Clovers will not thrive in acid land. Test your land with a soil kit and if the pH is below 6.5, bang on some lime. The clovers will love you – and the grasses will ultimately love them. In very light land, and on chalk, potash is sometimes deficient. This then, if analysis indicates, should be applied. All these were dealt with in Chapter 2.

The other thing that encourages the clovers is hard grazing. If the grasses are left to get too coarse and vigorous they will shade out the clovers. Graze hard – and preferably intermittently – and you will give the clovers more chance.

Renovating existing pasture

If you find rough existing permanent pasture in your holding, and wish to go on having grass there, I suggest you consider renovating the pasture rather than ploughing it up and re-seeding. For one thing, ploughing up and re-seeding takes a great deal of money nowadays, when grass and clover seed is so expensive. For another it is a pity to eliminate all those species of grasses, clovers and herbs that have shown that they can survive on your soil and in your climate, and thus may be more healthy and nutritious for stock – or hard-wearing as a lawn – than any introduced species.

It is amazing how rough old grassland can be restored by proper treatment. Proper treatment nearly always means – treating it rough. First graze the grass as hard as you can with adult cattle or cut it close with a mower. Then make an analysis of the soil and if it needs it put on lime and if it needs it phosphate. There is nothing to beat the old-fashioned 'basic slag' for the latter. If the land is acid, though, it is quite a good plan to dress it heavily with ground rock phosphate, leave for a year, and *then* lime heavily. Do not put rock phosphate and lime on together, because acidity is needed to release the phosphoric acid from the rock phosphate. If the land is alkaline (a pH of 6.5 or over), slag will serve you better: bone meal is good and so is superphosphate.

Now 'drastic harrow' any time between November and March. Drag, or get a contractor to drag, heavy and grievous harrows over your pasture. Drag all the old dead mat out of it. Drag disc harrows over it if you like. Do this in the autumn or early winter. Give it hell. Make it look as if it will never recover again. Next spring is the time, if you think perhaps the pasture lacks clover, to broadcast some seed over it. Eight pounds of cocksfoot and a pound of wild white clover on lighter land, or substitute Timothy for the cocksfoot on heavy land, is ideal. You can do this by hand on a small area, by seed-fiddle (see page 42) on a bigger, and by fertilizer spreader behind a big tractor on a very large area. Light harrow it after this. You can sometimes get 'cleanings' which is seed winnowed from pure seed. It is very cheap and perfectly adequate for 'renovating' pastures.

In the spring treat it more kindly. Graze it, preferably with cattle, and graze it intermittently: that is, let the cattle eat it right down then take them off for a couple of months to let it grow up again. Both grass and clover give of their best if bitten right down, then allowed to grow up to flowering stage again, then bitten or cut right down again. The period of rest allows them to develop a decent root system.

There should be a good harrowing in the autumn again – but a light harrowing this time, just enough to spread the dung. Hens allowed to run on pasture are excellent at spreading manure – also eating nasties. If there is a lot of grass in it when you shut it up for the winter, put some sheep on it, just for the winter. They will 'clean it up'. Next summer, if you want, you can shut the pasture up for hay. It will do it good then to cut it for hay or silage, which will depress the coarse and unpalatable grasses. But then put animals on it to graze the 'aftermath', which is what farmers call the growth after the hay has been cut. And, remember, if you take a cut of hay off a field you should put something back. Preferably a good dressing of muck, or farmyard manure (see chapter 2).

Do not let the pasture get coarse, tufty, or go to seed. Graze it or cut it before it does this. You may be surprised at turning, after a few years, what at first looked shocking old no-good rubbish into some of the best pasture imaginable – and that without the expense of buying a single seed. If you can afford it though, ploughing and re-seeding is quicker and generally better.

Now if you are faced with the same problem, but you do not wish to use animals, you must do your grazing by mechanical means. This really means, in modern terms, a rotary grass cutter. For cattle and sheep read a Flymo or equivalent on a tiny scale or a tractor-drawn implement on a larger. You can do just as good a job. If you find the rotary jibs at the very tough tussocks (as I am finding on some very tough grassland I am trying to tame at the moment), use one of those devices that you carry under your arm, slung from a harness, with a little motor at one end of it and a rotary blade at the other – a 'brush cutter'. That will slice through the toughest tussock that ever was. You will only need to use it once – what about hiring one?

But remember, if you just cut grass, and take it away, and don't put anything back, you are robbing the land. You *must* put something back. Animal manure is better than anything (just strew it about on top – the worms will drag it in). In default of that make compost with the grass you remove (and other material too) and spread that on. I would never recommend much in the way of inorganic manures – once you have corrected any serious deficit in lime, phosphorus, or potash. Organic manure is better in every way.

Renovating by re-seeding

If you *do* decide to plough-up-and-re-seed', or if you want to plant with a crop, there are several ways to do it. The advice commonly given to such people by neighbours or the advisory service is; spray it first with a herbicide, such as paraquat. The herbicide will destroy every living thing in that soil and you are left with an inert soil to begin again with.

I would never recommend such a practice, as it is quite against the rules of good husbandry, besides being nothing less than wholesale murder of other creatures. The only creatures you will be doing good to by such methods are the shareholders in the firm that produces the chemical – and you will be doing them a great deal of good, for the price of these poisons is enormous, and going ever upward by the month. It will be a good thing for true husbandry when they have priced themselves right out of the market.

THE LORE OF THE LAND

There are several much better, cleaner, safer and more humane methods of taming old pasture land, and it is only laziness, or lack of knowledge, that drives people to poison warfare.

One of the simplest method is, quite simply, *pigs*. If you confine pigs behind an electric fence on the old pasture you wish to convert they will eat all the grass, eat its roots (including all the roots of the dreaded couch grass), eat or kill creeping thistle roots, docks, and any other – to you – noxious weeds. And all these plants they will transform either into excellent bacon or excellent manure. They will waste not one jot of it, but leave your land far more fertile, and in far better heart, than it was before.

There are some caveats about this though, and here OMCS must be allowed full play. It is not good to put unringed pigs on land that is very heavy clay in wet weather, because they will puddle the clay. One small piggy-wig will *not* dig and manure for you, to any effect, a ten-acre field. You must concentrate your pigs – maybe six to a quarter of an acre – and be ready to move them on to another quarter of an acre the moment they have finished the job on the first one. It is good neither for land nor for pigs to leave pigs on a piece of land too long. What is 'too long'? Your observation – and your OMCS – must be the arbiters of this. When the land has been well and truly dug, cleared of weeds, and manured, move the pigs. If you have no more land to move them to, eat them, sell them, or shut them up in a sty. (If you don't want to do any of these things an alternative course is to ring their noses and turn them out on grassland: preferably ley pasture.)

This is not a book about keeping pigs but I must here remark that your pigs will not live on what they find on that land alone – you must feed them much as you would if they were indoors. They will thrive and wax prosperous and their shadows will not decrease.

If you don't want to go to the bother of pigs, another method is to graze the grassland right down in the summer (the animals that graze it will manure it for you too) or, in default of animals, cut it right short with a mower. Then plough it in the autumn or late summer. Plough it well – completely inverting it. Let it lie a fortnight and then *disc* it four or five times. (Discs are sharp steel discs set in a frame that are dragged over the land by horse or tractor.) Do *not* try to harrow it or cultivate it with a tine cultivator – if you do you will merely drag all that grass and rubbish to the surface again. Disc it, and for the first two passes of the discs run up and down the furrows not across them. Then, before the middle of October, broadcast winter rye seed over the land and lightly harrow it in and roll it too if you think it needs it.

The rye will grow all winter and will help to smother other grasses and the weeds. In the spring either graze off the rye and then plough it in, or, if you haven't got animals, just plough it in. The old grasses will have rotted down completely by then and returned their goodness to the soil and – that summer – you will have fertile and weed-free land to get going with.

By far the best way of establishing good grass, in my experience, is to plough the land in autumn after having grazed it very hard indeed the summer before, and to let it lie rough during the winter. The frost will help to break it down. The following spring, as soon as the land is dry enough, give it a pass or two (maybe three or four depending upon how much it needs) with the disc harrows, then a pass with light spiked harrows, then a pass with a rib roller (an invaluable instrument), then broadcast your seed; then pass the spiked harrow at right angles to the way the rib roller went, and, if you have one, give it a pass with the flat roller. And leave it at that. If you intend to lay down grass for several years it really does pay to do it well, and the above sequence of preparations is ideal. And get it down as early in the season as you can – as soon as the weather allows you to get tackle on the soil.

Of course this calls for a lot of equipment, but there are such things as contractors, and friendly neighbours. If you don't have a big farm it is far better to rely on these and not lay a lot of money out on equipment which you will only use occasionally.

The above advice applies to field-scale work of course: on a garden scale you can do exactly the same things, but for 'plough' read 'spade'; for 'discs' read 'mattock' or 'heavy hoe'. Above all do *not* do anything the first autumn that will tend to bring the old vegetative mat to the surface again.

Couch grass

or twitch, spear grass, knotgrass, etc.

If you are in a hurry, though, and wish to plant up some old grass-land *now*, the only way to do it, on a garden scale, is to skim the turf off with a spade and bury the turf, upside-down, at the bottom of each spade trench as you dig it. This is very effective, good for the land, but very hard on your back.

The other method for either field or garden is – rotovate – rotovate – rotovate. Rotovate until you've chewed everything up right small. Creeping weeds and docks will keep coming up again, but if you give them no peace – either hit them again with the rotovator or with spade, fork, or hoe – you will beat them in the end.

Personally, I'd rather let the piggies do the work.

Grasses, clovers and herbs

Now for a description of various species of grasses, clovers, and a third class of vegetables we haven't yet noticed – herbs. It is becoming more and more common, particulary with the growing army of organic farmers and gardeners (there is nothing like nitrogenous manure at over a hundred pounds a ton to make people think 'organic') to include seed of various edible and deep-rooting herbs in their leys or permanent pastures. This is good for the soil and even better for any animals that may graze it.

But we will start with grasses:

Perennial Rye Grass (*Lolium perenne*). This is the basis and hard core of most grass seed mixtures intended either for grazing or hay. It is highly productive and highly nutritious. It is very persistent, but – like many highly productive, highly bred things – needs good treatment, like lots of nitrogen. Plenty of clover in the pasture gives it this and will keep it going indefinitely. It is early, recovers well from grazing, and goes on late in the winter too.

Italian Rye Grass (*Lolium multiflorum*). This is the agribusinessman's darling, for it can be sown pure as a ley, with no clover, and flogged to enormous yields with massive applications of nitrogen. It is not a perennial but a biennial: if allowed to flower and seed it dies out after

a

b

c

d

e

f

g

a. crested dogstail

b. cocksfoot

c. sweet vernal

d. perennial ryegrass

e. italian ryegrass

f. timothy

g. meadow fescue

h. smooth-stalked meadow
                    grass

i. meadow foxtail

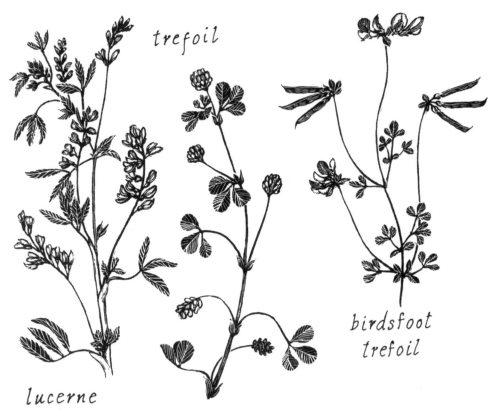

trefoil

birdsfoot
trefoil

lucerne

two years. If consistently grazed it will often last much longer, for if it is not allowed to flower it does not know it is two years old and goes on living. I have often found, too, that if it is in a seed mixture that is cut for hay it sheds its seed early and survives by seeding. But generally speaking it is a grass for short leys and not for long ones. Many people include it in longer leys though – or even in seedlings for permanent pasture – because it produces freely in the first two years, before the perennial grasses have established themselves. Not too much should be employed in the mixture though, for, when it does die out, it should not leave too big a gap. Six pounds of seed to the acre is the maximum; for permanent grassland I prefer a far lower amount, if any at all. But it **does** help, that first year, to give you a good bite, and it acts as a nurse crop to the perennial grasses.

Cocksfoot (*Dactylis glomerata*). This is one of the most valuable of our grasses. It is deep-rooting, very drough-resistant, very productive, early to bulk up, and very nutritious. Objections are levelled against it by people who say that it is coarse and unpalatable. It is only so if

red clover

alsike

white clover

it is mismanaged. When it occurs in a mixture, the herbage must be grazed hard, or, if it is for hay, cut early: as soon as the Cocksfoot is in flower. When it is past flowering it does become unpalatable and loses its nutritive value. In neglected, under-utilized pasture, it can become rampant and too dominant. But if properly managed it is the best of grasses for short-term ley or permanent pasture, for hay or grazing.

Meadow Fescue (Festuca pratensis). Much less aggressive than either the Rye grasses or Cocksfoot, it is therefore sown sometimes together with lucerne (alfalfa) or sometimes in association with Timothy. It is a very palatable and nutritious grass, very good on light, dry land, and I would be inclined to include it in most seed mixtures. Good for either grazing or mowing. It should be cut not later than flowering, but it flowers pretty late.

Tall Fescue (Festuca elatior). Very good for producing an early bite, good in heavy, wet soil but, surprisingly, also very drought-resistant. Like Cocksfoot, it is deep rooting. A valuable grass to sow, although not as palatable as some and slow to establish.

Hard Fescue *(Festuca Duriuscula)*. Used much in lawns, sports grounds and the like. Said to be drought-resistant and winter hardy. I would not use it for hay or pasture.

Timothy *(Phleum pratense)*. Much sown in the cold wet West of Britain but will grow anywhere, very productive and nutritious – an excellent grass to sow and should be included in every mixture, and particularly good as a mixture with clover. A nice thing about it is that it produces a lot of small seed and therefore its seed is much cheaper than that of any other grass. It doesn't like drought or very dry land. It yields very heavily in water meadows or under irrigation. You can go on grazing it late in the spring before shutting it up for hay and it will still give you a good crop of hay if it has enough moisture. After the hay cut it is very slow to 'come away' as farmers say, for the aftermath. *P. bertoloni* is a related species very good for grassing down orchards, sports grounds, and also used for re-seeding hill land.

Rough-Stalked Meadow Grass *(Poa trivialis)*. Should always be included in permanent pasture mixtures as it makes plenty of 'bottom' – that is, heavy herbage down near the ground. It increases the productiveness of pasture for grazing and helps, by its prostrate habit and thick mat, to keep out inferior grasses.

Smooth-Stalked Meadow Grass *(Poa pratensis)*. Has creeping roots (actually underground stems) which make it very drought-resistant, and is therefore planted on dry sandy soils in dry climates. Otherwise only sown for lawns and sports grounds because it is tough and hard wearing.

Meadow Foxtail *(Alopecurus pratensis)*. One of the very finest of grasses for permanent pasture: early, palatable and productive. It takes several years to come into full production, though, and it is therefore not worth sowing it in short term leys. It should always be included in permanent pasture.

Crested Dogstail *(Cynosurus cristatus)*. Used a lot in sports grounds because it is very hard wearing. Not much good for high-class lawns (too wiry), no good for hay. Sown sometimes on high sheep pastures but has a modest yield.

So now we come to clovers:

Wild White Clover (Trifolium repens). By far the most important clover in Northern Europe, and you probably get it whether you want it or not. In the rainier areas it will come into pasture without being sown or introduced and, if the land is alkaline enough (limed) and there is sufficient phosphate, it will spread. You can increase it in relation to the grasses by three methods: adding lime (if necessary), adding phosphates, and hard grazing. Hard grazing early in the spring particularly favours it, because it does not show itself until late spring and therefore escapes this attention, while the early and vigorous grasses – notably rye grass and cocksfoot – are bitten back. Conversely sparing the pasture in the spring, or not grazing it too heartily, and grazing only intermittently in the summer, so as to allow the tall grasses to go ahead, suppresses Wild White. It is necessary to suppress it sometimes, because it can become so rampant as to overcome the grasses and, being late starting and early ending (remember that clovers are not persistent in our winter and give no winter grazing), this lessens the value of the pasture. But it must never be forgotten, particularly by organic farmers and gardeners, that the clovers give us *free nitrogen*, and generally I find myself trying to encourage them at the expense of the grasses rather than the other way round.

New Zealand Wild White Clover and *Kentish Wild White Clover* are strains of Wild White. The first tends to be cheaper, but the second, if certified and supplied by a good merchant, is very reliable.

Dutch White Clover is much used for short-term leys, but not for long ones or permanent pasture, where Wild White is preferred.

Red Clover (Trifolium pratense). Early Red Clover (or Broad-Leaved Red) gives an earlier cut or bite than Late Flowering Red which we shall consider, but it is not so persistent. It is used in short-term leys; when used in longer leys it is included simply to provide an early bite in the first year or two. It tends to die out after three years.

Late Flowering Red Clover (Trifolium pratense perenne). Far more use for longer leys or permanent pasture because it is persistent. It flowers about three weeks after Early Red.

Alsike Clover (Trifolium hybridium). Was introduced from Sweden over a century ago. It grows where the Red Clovers will not: in wet and boggy land, acid land (up to a point) and land which is subject to 'clover sickness'. It persists for three or four years only and is therefore more suitable for short leys. Mixed, pure, with Timothy, it makes a good and bulky hay crop.

Trefoil (Medicago lupulina). Also called Nonsuch Clover. Not very persistent, being an annual, but will sometimes self-seed. Much used on very light, or very calcareous, soils for short leys.

Bird's Foot Trefoil (Lotus corniculatus). A perennial and very good plant to grow on light, sandy soils. Very drought-resistant.

Lucerne or *Alfalfa (Medicago sativa).* One of the very important fodder crops in the world, but not in Britain. In hot, dry countries, under irrigation, it gives enormous yields of highly nutritious fodder, makes magnificent hay, can be grazed, and is frequently put through a hammer mill for the production of lucerne meal. I have seen *seven* heavy hay cuts a year in the Karroo area of South Africa, under heavy irrigation.

In Europe, the further you go south, the more lucerne you will see. In the British Isles it has proved very valuable in dry sandy areas, such as the Brecklands of Suffolk and Norfolk. We grew it to great effect on our sandy land in East Suffolk. But in British conditions it cannot stand too long the competition of native weeds and grasses, and will inevitably become choked out in the end, although, in the right climate, it is a very long-lived perennial. Its roots go to unbelievable depths and therefore it is extremely drought-resistant. To establish it, you must make sure your land is quite clean (perennial weeds will quickly choke it); you must sow well after the latest frost, and you must make sure the seed is inoculated (by the seed merchant) with the right bacteria to form nodules on its roots.

Now for the knotty problem of **seed mixtures**.

When I was a boy, farmers sowed very complex seed mixtures, in the pious hope that even if everything didn't come up, some would. After the Second World War seed mixtures became enormously simplified; many of them became just two or three strains of Rye Grass and Wild White Clover and nothing else. Some farmers even omitted the clover and just piled on huge applications of nitrogenous fertilizer. But now, with dearer nitrogen, and increasing sense, there is a move back to mixtures containing more varieties. My own predilection is for plenty of variety, because I believe in copying the complexity of Nature. I believe firmly, too, in including some deep rooting herbs – neither grasses nor clovers, and I give descriptions of a few of these in due course.

The old and tried 'Cockle Park Mixture' was:
16lb per acre of Perennial Rye Grass
10lb per acre of Cocksfoot
4lb per acre of Timothy
1lb per acre of Trefoil
1½ lb per acre of Wild White Clover
(36½ lb per acre in total)

This mixture was generally sown under a 'cover' or 'nurse' crop, which will be discussed later. If a cover crop was not used, up to 10lb of Italian Rye Grass would have been added to this; my own feeling is that this is too much: 5lb would be better. (It is most important, incidentally, when growing a new seed mixture under, as it were, an Italian Rye Grass cover that the Italian Rye Grass should be grazed off before it grows too rampant and suppresses the perennials.)

On very rough, poor land, such as ploughed-up moorland, a common mixture is:
28lb per acre of Perennial Rye Grass
8lb per acre of Crested Dogstail
2lb per acre of Wild White Clover
(38lb per acre in total)

On wet, peaty land:
20lb per acre of Timothy
6lb per acre of Late Flowering Red Clover
2lb per acre of Wild White Clover
(28lb per acre in total)

Now we come to discuss specifically *herbal leys*: leys with deep-rooting, edible herbs in them such as are planted by that growing number of people who follow the Organic Philosophy.

That great prophet of the Organic Movement, the late Friend Sykes, who farmed successfully and extremely profitably for most of his lifetime without using an ounce of artificial fertilizer or poison sprays, and who consistently outproduced all his chemically farming neighbours, used to sow the following mixture:

5lb per acre of Cocksfoot
5lb per acre of Perennial Rye Grass
1lb per acre of Italian Rye Grass
3lb per acre of Timothy
1lb per acre of Rough-Stalked Meadow Grass
1lb per acre of Crested Dogstail
1lb per acre of White Clover (Aberystwyth S.100)
3lb per acre of Late Flowering Red Clover
1lb per acre of Alsike
3lb per acre of Lucerne
3lb per acre of American Sweet Clover
10lb per acre of Sainfoin
3lb per acre of Burnet
2lb per acre of Chicory
½ lb per acreof Yarrow
(41½ lb per acre in total)

sainfoin

This very complex mixture of plants was left down for four years, and grazed during that time with a great mixture of animals: Guernsey dairy cows, Galloway beef cattle, half-bred ewes crossed with a Suffolk ram, poultry, and thoroughbred horses. All these animals were famous for their health and fitness and no vet ever made any sort of a living off Chantry Farm. The health record of the stock, once the system had been established a few years, was excellent. Friend Sykes copied nature by having a great variety of living things: many species of both plants and animals. One species makes up for another's defects. No disease organism can get a hold, for each pathogen can only attack one species and there is always another species ready to come along and gobble it up. One species of animal will eat what is avoided by another species. Deep-rooting herbs draw sustenance

plantain
or
ribgrass

burnet

yarrow

chicory

from deep down in the sub-soil and ultimately this sustenance, after being consumed and excreted by animals, goes into the topsoil for the use of the shallow-rooting species. Thus is health of soil, plant, animals and Man slowly but steadily built up.

America Sweet Clover in the above mixture seems to me to be an unnecessary complication. Of the herbs, **Sainfoin** (*Onobrychis viciae-folia*) is a valuable fodder plant, rich in protein, cobalt, magnesium, phosphorus and other trace elements. **Burnet** (*Poterium sanguisorba*) is a very deep-rooting, drought-resistant herb with most valuable dietetic properties. **Chicory** (*Cichorium intybus*) is a fine herb (it is interesting to see how cows will go straight for it, proving that they need it). It must be grazed hard or it gets too high and rampant, and it can be a little difficult in hay, for it is hard to dry. It comes very early in the season. **Yarrow** (*Achillea millefolium*) is highly medicinal, to humans as to cows and sheep. It is spectacularly drought-resistant, putting down very strong roots. It is high in protein.

A herb not included in Friend Sykes' mixture is **Ribgrass** (*Plantago lanceolata*). This is sometimes sown with seed mixtures. I would not recommend it. It seems to choke out too many other grasses and is not very palatable.

Now a word about 'nurse crops'.

Nurse crops

A time hounoured practice is to sow grass-and-clover seeds under another (arable) crop. The crop is then harvested, leaving the new ley exposed to the light of day and whatever the farmer intends to do with it. The nurse crop was generally corn, such as barley or oats sown in spring. Wheat is a bad nurse crop: it takes too much out of the soil and starves the grasses. The practice is to drill a spring corn crop and then, a day or two after, broadcast your ley seeds (see pages 43 and 44) and give a light harrowing. The theory is that you waste no time like this: you get a corn crop and as soon as it is harvested in the stock can go to a fresh lively new bite of grass.

My own experience points to the advantage of *not* sowing grasses under a corn crop at all. The corn crop, with a seed mixture under it, will not yield as well as it would have done, and the subsequent ley is likely to be of poorer quality.

It is better to sow a ley mixture in the spring with no nurse crop, except perhaps some Italian Rye Grass, or (and this is very good) a light seeding of Rape (say 4lb to the acre), and then get stock onto the land early in the summer: perhaps two months after sowing the seed. This makes good use of the land that summer (you may lose the nurse barley or oats crop, but you do get a summer's grazing) and the treading and nibbling of the animals improves the 'tillering' (spreading out of) the grass and clover plants and ensures a better and a cleaner ley. Many more farmers are coming round to this view nowadays. If you have reason to believe your land is foul (i.e. full of weeds) then take a 'half fallow' and sow your seeds in mid-August. True, you miss a summer, but the half fallow gives you a chance to destroy the weeds. Half fallowing means ploughing and cultivating and harrowing and otherwise disturbing the land as many times as you can during the first part of the summer. This destroys the weeds. With this August sowing you can include 4lb of Rape seed with the grass-and-clover and graze this off in the autumn and early winter. This feeds the stock and the treading helps the ley.

Grazing grassland

The after-treatment of grassland is important. If you really wish to get the most value from it then you must play it very skilfully.

The points to remember are:

- Heavy grazing *early* in the season will suppress the better grasses and encourage the clovers, but if done too often will encourage weed grasses (Yorkshire Fog, Bents, etc.).
- Inadequate stocking will depress the clovers and the better grasses and encourage the weeds and coarse grasses.
- Grazing the herbage right down all the year gives nothing a chance to develop a proper root system and will eventually destroy good pasture.
- The best method of grazing is to graze right down, then rest until the grasses are six to nine inches high, then graze right down again.

- It is best to grow some very early crop (Rye is the best I know - Winter Rye, particular one of the Polish varieties) for your early bite so as to spare your grassland until well into May – then graze *hard*, rest, graze hard again, and so on. If the clovers appear to be losing the battle, then graze earlier the next spring. If the good grasses are losing to the clovers, graze later in the spring, and then give more rest during the summer.

Paddock grazing is no doubt the best method. For this, if you have enough land, fence it into at least six paddocks, and all must have a water supply. Put your milking cows into a paddock first and let them cream off the best of it. After say a week move them into the next paddock and put, say, bullocks and sheep into the first one. After a week move them all on. In theory in six weeks' time the cows will go into the first paddock again. If you only have a few acres, two or three paddocks are better than none.

The effect of different kinds of **stock** on land is important. Cows want long grass and clover, and the best of it. Sheep will follow cows – never the other way round. Sheep will nibble quite close (cows graze by wrapping their tongues around grass and therefore need long grass, sheep nip it off very short). Horses will accompany, or go after, sheep. They are very close grazers. Land with nothing but horses on always deteriorates. They are terribly fussy feeders, leaving great tufts of grass, and always dung in one place. Horses mixed with other stock do good.

Geese are very good grazers. It is said their droppings make the grass unpalatable for other stock. I don't believe this lasts very long.

Sows will graze well. On new ley pasture, if moved often enough, they will graze even if they are not ringed. The moment they begin to get their snouts into the ground, though, either move them or ring them. But if you want to clear rough land with them, do not ring them at all.

Hens will do pasture good if not over-concentrated. Fifty hens to an acre will do nothing but good.

Goats are browsers not grazers. They will eat grass and clover but prefer the leaves and shoots of bushes, trees, and lots of other things. They will turn a semi-desert into a desert quicker than any other animal; they can kill quite large trees and will never suffer a baby tree to grow up. Used properly, though, they do a great job. They will clear scrubland, consume thistles and other 'weeds' (deriving great benefit from them), and give you fine milk, the very best of cheese, and the billy kids make wonderful curry.

It is generally reckoned that good grassland, in good heart, should support a cow-equivalent to the acre. A large horse can be considered as a cow-and-a-half equivalent, a pony as one cow equivalent; sheep go six to the cow-equivalent, or five large ones. But it must be remembered that with mixed grazing you can keep more stock to the acre than you can with one-species grazing. It is generally assumed (from my experience correctly) that if you are grazing a given number of cows on a piece of land, you can introduce the same number of sheep and they will survive and the cows will not suffer. The sheep 'clean up' after the cows and the pasture will benefit. Thus if you have 20 cows on a piece of land and they are doing well, you can add 20 sheep and they will do well too and the cows will do no worse.

Of course if you graze rotationally the sheep should always *follow* the cows – not the other way about.

Geese will graze well after cows also, and so will horses. Land grazed with horses only – as in the 'horseyculture' areas of the Home Counties – invariably suffers, and so do the horses. Horses, above all other animals, require mixed grazing to flourish – and not too many horses to an acre. You get fierce worm-build-ups on heavily horsed land.

Now if, as probably happens, you suddenly find your grass 'running away from you' in June or early July – in other words if it is growing too fast and your animals cannot keep up with it – then you must cut some, and conserve it for hay or silage.

The trouble with grass (and even more with clover) in northern climates is that it is terribly seasonal. In June you can bang in five cows to an acre and they won't keep pace with it; in August one cow will be too much for it and in winter none. In winter cows are best kept off the land, unless they be put on arable fodder crops like kale. But sheep do good to grassland in the winter, cleaning it up and treading and manuring it. Dry cattle, and cows with calves at foot, will out-winter, given a little hay to help them on, but watch that they do not poach the pasture too badly.

So really the rationale of all this is that you must keep enough stock to graze your grass down really hard in summer time – and then conserve enough grass to feed them during the winter. Or else sell 'em in the autumn, either fat or as 'stores' for somebody else to fatten.

Ideally, one should chain harrow grassland fairly often during the summer and spike harrow once in the winter.

Hay-making

It is vital to cut your grass for hay before it gets too old! It is almost true to say that the younger it is the better it is. Once it is past flower-ing it very quickly loses all its feeding value. Once it has seeded, it is only good for bedding. Besides, if you leave grass to grow that long it will kill the clover and ruin the pasture. Cut it before it flowers – or just after.

The art then is to dry it – without knocking all the leaves off it – enough so that it does not heat in the stack and go bad; but not too much, or you will lose much of the leaf.

The pick-up baler has revolutionized haymaking. Before its advent we used to 'make' our hay with wooden rakes and pitch-forks, or horse-drawn tedders if we were bang up to date (i.e. cut the grass and then leave to dry in the wind and sun, turning several times); we then used to 'cock' it (pile it into heaps about five foot in diameter at the base and seven foot high). Then, after the cocks had stood in the field a few days, we would load the hay on to wagons, drag it to the stackyard, stack it and thatch it. All these operations required skill, knowledge and plenty of OMCS.

Nowadays the grass is cut – generally with a rotary mower – and im-mediately flung about by a tractor-drawn tedder; as soon as it's dry,

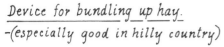

Device for bundling up hay.
-(especially good in hilly country)

wooden peg with drilled hole for cord & notches

push peg into ground & lay out cord. place heap of loose hay on top near peg ~

peg

take loose ends over heap & under notches in peg~ hold peg down with foot & pull ~ tie loose ends~ now you have a handy bundle for carrying.

along comes the pick-up baler, like a great grass-eating and bale-excreting monster, bales it up into tight heavy bales, we fling these up on to trailers and take them back to the hay barn. They take up much less space than loose hay, and can be carted in a fraction of the time.

But, in my opinion, it is nothing like such good hay. I believe many of us have forgotten what really fine, high-class hay is like.

On a small scale I strongly advise the **tripod method**. You make a tripod by taking three six-foot (or thereabouts – they don't have to be exact) poles (I have seen broomsticks used in Scotland!), standing them up to form a tripod, with a simple loop of cord or string to tie their tops together, dropping two or three different-sized loops of wire over them to form parallel members; then lay three 'hutches', made by bending corrugated iron at an angle so as to make a tent-shaped form, against the three legs, piling up the hay the day after

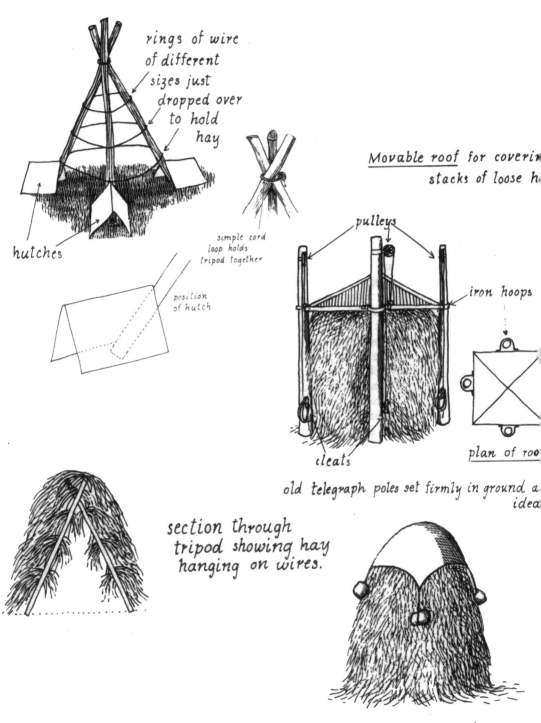

Tripod *for drying small quantities of hay.*

rings of wire
of different
sizes just
dropped over
to hold
hay

hutches

simple cord
loop holds
tripod together

position
of hutch

Movable roof *for coverin*
stacks of loose h

pulleys

iron hoops

plan of roo

cleats

old telegraph poles set firmly in ground a
idea

section through
tripod showing hay
hanging on wires.

cap on haycock.

it is cut *very loosely* around the tripod, keeping the sides vertical and topping it with a nice dome eight or nine feet high. Then withdraw the 'hutches' to be used on the next tripod. Their withdrawal will leave air vents for the air to get in. You will need from six to eight tripods per acre. A refinement is to fit a little canvas or plastic cap over each one.

Quite green hay can be tripoded, and left for several days before carting. It will be far better hay than grass which has been kicked violently about in the field half a dozen times to dry it, by force as it were, which knocks all the clover leaves out of it. Done properly, tripoding is far the best way of making hay.

But I do advise you – ask a friendly neighbour to help and advise with your hay-making if you are inexperienced. Nothing can take the place of years of practice when knowing how to treat grass and detecting when it is ready to come to the baler or the wagon. If you stack or bale damp or green grass, it will go mouldy, your stock won't thrive, and you can get farmer's lung – a horrible disease. If you stack it too dry, you will lose much of its nutritive value. Leaving it too long in the sun is bad for it.

Silage is another excellent way of conserving the summer flush of grass. Silage is grass or other greenstuff cut when 10-12" high, as many times as possible throughout the summer, allowed to wilt in the field for a day at most, carted to the silage stack, packed in and stamped or rolled and then kept resolutely from all air and water. The stuff ferments, lactic acid being formed by bacteria, and the high acidity keeps it from rotting. It is much the same process as the making of sauerkraut. Surprisingly it is very palatable and highly nutritious.

Some farmers add molasses to the greenstuff as they put it down and this cannot but be helpful. Twenty pounds of molasses, diluted in an equal amount of water, is sprinkled on each ton of green matter or thereabouts. Fermentation is encouraged and quality improved.

Nowadays alkathene sheeting, carefully wrapped round the material, keeps the air out. Generally a tractor drives up and down on the stack first to consolidate it. Often old motor tyres are flung on top of the alkathene to weight it down. Only if air and water are kept completely out will you get good silage.

In Norway smallholders make what they call **very high quality silage,** by packing the stuff carefully in towers, where there is no danger from air or water.

You can make silage in any weather. A little grass can be added every day for weeks if necessary. You should not add too much at once: it is better if each dollop heats a bit before the next one is dumped on top of it.

Hay-making can be done with fairly simple equipment. All you really need is a mower of some kind (a scythe is not impossible: a good man with a sharp scythe can mow an acre a day), a pitchfork, a hay rake, and a pair of strong arms. For silage you really need some sort of forage harvester with a tractor to draw it – although silage was made in the days of horses too. Personally I am a hay man: I agree with Bottom in *Midsummers Night's Dream*: 'Good hay hath no fellow!'

Weeds of grassland

Bracken. Bracken which can take over pasture, will only do so on under-stocked pasture. It can be completely eliminated in two or three seasons by concentrating mature cattle on it during the spring months when it is just coming up. The cattle nibble the young shoots (and do *not* die of bracken poisoning) and trample the plants to death. I have had direct experience of this several times and know it works. But the cattle must be fairly concentrated, and it must be in the spring.

Thistles. These can be eliminated by repeated cutting or bruising. When I was young I was taught an old rhyme: 'Cut thistles in June and you've cut 'em too soon. Cut 'em in July – they may die. Cut' 'em in August – die they must.' This has truth in it, but the trouble is that if you cut 'em in August they may have already seeded. The best thing to do is to cut 'em in all three of those months. No matter how tough and extensive the roots are of any dicotyledon plant, it cannot stand constant cutting or bruising, particularly while it is growing

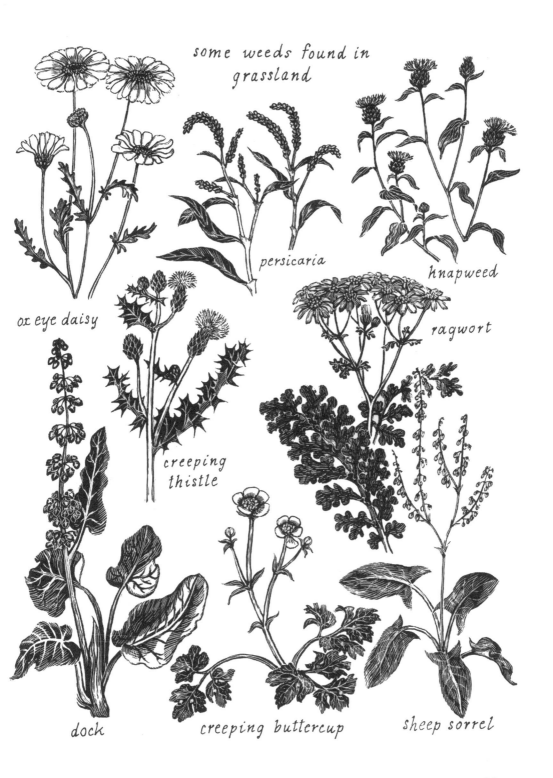

some weeds found in grassland

persicaria

knapweed

ox eye daisy

ragwort

creeping thistle

dock

creeping buttercup

sheep sorrel

vigorously in the early part of the season.

Thistles are biennials of course, and have a flat ground-hugging habit their first year and then it's very hard to cut 'em at all, so, to kill them by the cutting treatment, you have got to repeat the treatment for at least two years.

Cutting a field for hay every now and then, *before* the thistles have seeded, effectually controls them.

Bashing with a forage harvester of the flail type is even better than cutting. Donkeys and goats will both get rid of thistles.

Docks. I like to see a few docks in grassland: they are very deep-rooting and thus bring trace elements and other goodies up from the subsoil. Stock will nibble them, and if grassland is well stocked, and cut occasionally for hay, docks soon cease to be a problem. 'Weeds' are so often a 'problem' only because they are a problem in our minds. If we believed clover was a 'weed', clover would be a problem. But certainly docks should not be allowed to get out of hand. The good old 'dock spud' (a small steel blade on the end of stick) carried when you go for a walk over your acres is a very good control.

Nettles. Should not be a problem on properly managed pasture. If they are, repeated cutting will kill them, when cut, they are eaten by animals.

Creeping Buttercups. Liming helps to keep pasture free of buttercups, but they can take over, in which case the only remedy is to plough up and re-seed.

Ragwort. This is very unpopular stuff and even the greatest of weed-lovers finds it hard to defend. Cattle and horses will not touch it when it's growing, and when cut, and perhaps present in hay, it is actually poisonous. Fortunately, though, sheep love it when it is young, and by grazing sheep on it in the early summer you will completely eliminate it – probably in one season, certainly in two. I have never known this fail. Failing sheep, pulling, before it seeds, is a very good remedy. You can be forced in law by your neighbours to remove ragwort, thistles and some other weeds from your land.

Poisons. There is, of course, a deadly array of poisons to deal with weeds, all very expensive. Some are supposed to be 'selective', that is, they kill the weed you hate but not the crop you love. All life being one they invariably damage the crop to some extent too. Many are claimed by their makers (who charge an awful lot of money for them) to be transient or non-persistent.

My feeling about them is that I would never use them; I would never advise anybody else to use them; and I think, on land holdings of a sensible size (i.e. not huge ones), their employment is quite unjustifiable. All weeds can be controlled perfectly easily by mechanical or manual means or proper grassland control. Remember, every time you put a poison on the land, you are poisoning somebody's water supply. Perhaps your own. For it all gets washed down into the aquifer below.

Pests

Rabbits. Out of control, rabbits are a terrible pest; in reasonable numbers they are pleasant to have and are delicious in a pie with a piece of fat bacon in it. But the only reason why so many of us have been able to plant trees successfully during the last thirty years is the fact that myxomatosis (a disease that is enzootic to the Cottontail Rabbit of North America but became epizootic when introduced in Europe) wiped out most of our rabbit numbers. The bunny is coming back, and we must brace ourselves for it; but is is taking a long time. Every time we say: 'Look – the rabbits are back!' along comes another bout of 'myxy' and wipes most of 'em out again!

Rabbits would never have become a plague if most of their predators had not been wiped out. The pheasant craze of the eighteenth and nineteenth centuries, and the first half of this one, caused landlords to wage a relentless war against foxes, stoats, weasels and all birds of prey. The very means employed to destroy rabbits actually encouraged them – the gin trap. Men earned a living all over England and Wales setting hundred of these devices; they did catch millions of rabbits, but the gin set for the rabbit was deadly also against the rabbit's enemies: foxes, stoats and weasels. The latter were practically wiped out. Thus the rabbit reached plague proportions.

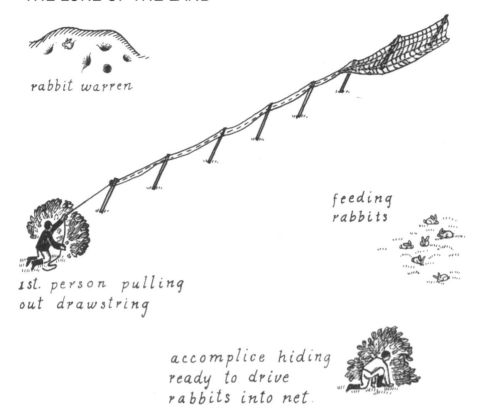

rabbit warren

feeding rabbits

1st. person pulling out drawstring

accomplice hiding ready to drive rabbits into net.

If the rabbit does 'come back' we must control his numbers but not those of this enemies. By far the best and most humane ways of keeping rabbit numbers down are by the long net and by ferrets. Long netting has been revolutionized by the invention of the nylon monofilament net such as is used for taking (generally illegally) sea trout or salmon. Such a net, from 4 to 6 inches across the mesh, set up on light stakes as in Sally's illustration, held up by a draw string, positioned between the rabbit warren and the rabbit's feeding ground, and left for a few days until the denizens get used to it, then dropped by the pulling out of a draw string, and the rabbits then started by a shout or the clapping of one's hands beyond them, will reap a harvest. Ferreting too is a good way of clearing rabbits, and, if you do it often enough, the survivors will go away and it will be some time before they come back. Wiring or snaring always seems to me cruel, you catch the poor old cat as well as the rabbits, and anyway you don't catch enough to make any difference in the numbers. Gassing with cyanide, or any other poison, is nothing less than revolting. Firstly you waste what is after all a very good human food, secondly

Netting Rabbits.

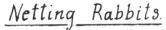

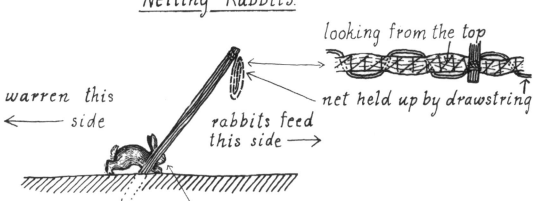

looking from the top

warren this
← *side*

rabbits feed
this side →

net held up by drawstring

rabbits get used to passing under net

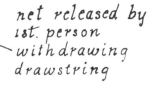

net released by
1st. person
withdrawing
drawstring

rabbit, frightened by
2nd. person, runs in
panic towards warren

the rabbit gets
tangled up in
loosely hanging net.

the most suitable net is $4\frac{1}{2}$" mesh green
nylon monofilament, at least 50 yds. long
and a yard and a half wide.

you cause disgusting suffering: many rabbits are not killed by the gas but maimed and made to suffer, and the sufferings of gassed rabbits before they die must be horrible. Surely we humans need not sink to this?

And yet bunny must be controlled, otherwise all tree-planting is in vain, unless expensive fencing and rabbit-clearing are undertaken, farming is difficult and market gardening is out.

Foxes. I used to shoot foxes but do not do so any more, because I am now convinced they do far more good than harm. They eat great numbers of field voles, which destroy grasses, they control rabbits, and they help to preserve the balance of nature. They eat hens? Then shut up your hens.

Moles. It is annoying to have a row of young seedlings uprooted by a mole. Try pushing the seedlings gently back and treading the ground firm again. It is annoying to see good grassland half covered with mole heaps. Use the chain harrow more often, or on a smaller scale spread the mole hills with a rake. Pretend it is good fertilizer, which it is. But if they really get you down and just become intolerable, attach a hose pipe to the exhaust of your motorbike, car, rotovator or other petrol engine, push the other end of it down a mole hill, and run the engine, preferably slightly choked. It may not kill the moles but it will be some time before they will come back. Personally I have long ago given up worrying about moles. Their existence used to drive me mad. Now I suffer them and they suffer me and neither of us really does the other any serious harm.

As for planting the 'mole-repellent plant' – caper spurge – forget it. The only time I tried it the moles came and pushed it out of the ground.

Rats. Your Warfarin hath no fellow. You have *got* to get rid of rats, for they really are a menace to mankind. They are just too like ourselves, in tastes and in habits. Buy Warfarin from the shop and mix it yourself with bait (flour, or any meal, will do), or buy it, slightly more expensively, already mixed, and – this is a good tip – mix some sugar with it. Put it in a dry place, such as inside an old drainpipe. And use *enough* of it. Do not let the rats go short of it. Put perhaps a teacupful of it in each station first. When it is gone put more. Be generous. It is *meanness* that has brought about the dreaded Warfarin-resistant rat. People half-fed the rats, it didn't kill them, and they developed an immunity. But don't worry about that – Warfarin generally works. If it doesn't, call the Pest officer in, and he will use something else.

But cleanliness, tidiness, and really reat-proof food storage is the best defence there is. And plenty of cats.

Grey Squirrels. Sadly, these can become a pest because they eat the growing points out of trees. I fancy, though, that they do most damage in huge plantations, and in woods of more reasonable proportions are not too bad. Two men with shot-guns, walking so that they fetch up on both sides of a tree, can shoot any squirrel on that tree because the poor little fellow cannot hide. Shooting at the drays, or nests, of grey squirrels is practised, as is also poking drays with long bamboo poles. I don't worry about grey squirrels unless they really give me substantial cause. After all, the odd deformed tree here and there is no matter – we cannot all be perfect. Of course there is a special place in Hell reserved for he who kills a red squirrel.

But the best attitude to pests is: we mustn't let any other animal make fools of us; but, subject to that proviso, the best policy is live and let live.

Chapter Four

Walls, Hedges, Fences and Gates

Wire is a fairly recent invention and has changed the history of the world. It has enabled Western man to settle large areas of the Earth's surface, over which he could but roam with his flocks and herds in the days before this invention.

But wire becomes more and more expensive; although we will discuss various forms of wire fence in due course, we will consider as well the alternatives. These in the past have been, chiefly, the thorn hedge in lowland areas, and the stone wall in upland. We will consider the latter first.

Stone walls

Stone walls are only really effective in controlling stock if you have unlimited access to good stone: that means 'freestone', that is, stone that naturally breaks out with at least two parallel sides. The oolitic limestone of the Cotswolds is famous for this, and therefore very good stock-proof stone walls surround – or *used* to surround – the fields of the Cotswold country. Alas, many of them have been bulldozed out in recent decades to allow the new agribusiness methods of get-rich-quick gentlemen, many have fallen down, and many have got untidy straggly bits of barbed wire atop of them, but the art of dry-stone-walling has not yet died, and some landowners valiantly keep alive the old traditions. As wire gets more and more expensive, more of them will.

The carboniferous limestones which make up much of the North of England also make good stone walls, and it is mind-boggling to observe the thousands and thousands of miles of good, solid stone-walling that our forefathers threw up on the Pennines and other

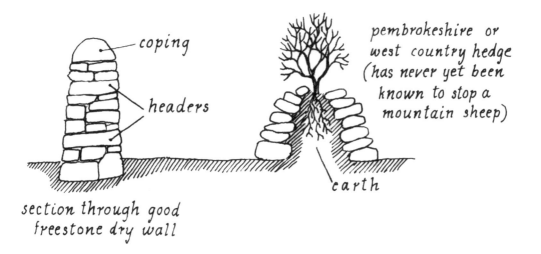

coping

headers

section through good
freestone dry wall

pembrokeshire or
west country hedge
(has never yet been
known to stop a
mountain sheep)

earth

places. In Wales Ordovician and Silurian shales are not as good but not too bad. In Pembrokeshire we have to make do with rough old pieces of Preseli Bluestone, all shapes and sizes, and to make a sheep-proof wall with them is extremely difficult. What we make instead are what are locally called 'hedges'. These are high banks with earth cores and stone-facing on both sides, with thorn hedges growing on top. In almost no case that I know of are such 'hedges' proof against Welsh Mountain sheep, and nearly all have to be surmounted by a wire fence. They serve principally, if the truth were known, to get rid of the boulders which most of us are constantly dragging out of our land. In the West Country you get the same thing.

But if you have access to good freestone you can build a beautiful and completely stock-proof wall. There is no secret in it, although to do it well takes skill and practice. The first essential is a good foundation. This is achieved by digging a trench down to hard soil. Then you need two strings to act as guide-lines, as with ordinary brick-laying. Then you must lay the stones skilfully so that all joints are broken (as shown in the illustration), and some larger stones go right through the wall from side to side. In other words, as a bricklayer would say, you must have some 'headers' as well as 'stretchers'. Look carefully at old stone walls in your district and copy them.

Thorn hedges

Thorn hedges are a very old device indeed. Hottentots in Namibia make *kraals* for their cattle by dragging cut thorn bushes into a circle – and men have probably done just this for thousands of years. The **quick-thorn hedge** ('quick'meaning living), which in Northern Europe should only mean one species of bush hawthorn (*Crataegus monogyna* and *C. oxanthoides*), is the permanent solution. All sorts of suggestions are made in books for other species of hedging plants, but in practice none of them is as good as hawthorn; it is the only hedge that really and consistently keeps stock out. There are a hundred ornamental hedge species, of course: holly, beech, box, yew, cyprus and many others. But if it's stock you want to keep in or out, choose hawthorn and nothing else. There is a kind of hawthorn called Plum-Leaved Thorn (*Crategus prunifolia*), with very tough thorns, which stands up well to urban pollution and vandals, but *oxanthoides* or *monogyna* – the two common-or-garden hawthorn or whitethorn plants of hedgerows all over the British Isles –are really your boys.

If you want to plant your own seed, you must gather haws in the autumn, before the birds do, and store them for eighteen months in damp sand. Then sow them in a seed-bed and transplant the tiny plants, when a year old, to a holding-bed, where they stay for another year or two before being planted out in the hedge. When planting as a hedge, put them nine inches apart in two rows which are nine inches apart too. OMCS would of course tell us to stagger them – so that each plant would be opposite a gap in the other row.

Now here is the rub. A young thorn hedge has to be protected from stock for a couple of years after it has been planted, otherwise it will be eaten. This means that, often, you have to build two temporary fences, one each side. If it were not for this fact, thorn hedges would be more common, because they would be cheaper than wire fences. As the price of wire zooms ever higher, maybe some bright person will invent a cheap method of protecting baby thorn hedges; if that happened, our countryside would quickly look better and a million song birds would sing his or her praise.

Meanwhile, there is nothing for it – you either have to erect a 'dead hedge' each side of your new quick hedge (as the ancients used to do) or put a temporary wire (probably netting) fence each side. A dead hedge is made by digging a small trench, standing in it thorn bushes which have been cut from an existing hedge, and tamping the earth into a trench to hold them up. Properly made, it will remain stock-proof long enough to allow the new quick-thorn to establish itself. For the first two years the young hedge should be weeded.

This done, after about five or six years, you will probably find your quick-thorn hedge needs attending to.

Everybody seems to think you inevitably have to *lay* a thorn hedge to keep it stock-proof. Actually, if the hedge is a good one in the first place, if you 'buck-head' it every year or two (cut it down to a suitable height), and 'flash' it (slash the small twigs off it: give it a haircut, in other words), and while doing so try to train it into a roughly pyramidal shape, your hedge may remain stock-proof for a hundred years or more (which is *far* longer than any wire fence is going to last).

Now a word here about mechanical hedge-cutting devices. These receive the blanket condemnation of all good country-lovers, but this is not altogether fair. True, there is a device which does not cut a hedge but *savages* it. It flails it – leaving a pathetic sight of shattered and mangled branches, and there is no doubt that no little trees in the world are going to withstand this treatment year after year for long. God knows, the hawthorn tree is hardy, and will stand up to abuse, but this sort of abuse is impossible to survive. These machines are much beloved of County Council surveyors, who perhaps know just what they are doing and *want* the hedge to die, only want it to seem like an act of God. It is not an act of God – it is an act of the Devil.

But there is another sort of machine, with a revolving blade, that cuts the branches through quite cleanly. If this is used in the correct manner it will not harm the hedge. The correct manner is: make the first cut lower than you want the top of the hedge to be. This first cut will be drastic, and cut through big branches, but it will be the last time you have to do this. Thereafter, every year (or two) you cut a couple of inches or more *higher* than that first cut. Thus you only prune off new growth and this does not damage the hedge. It does, though, force the hedge to put out more growth *lower down*, which is where you want it, to make a stock-proof hedge. No machine can ever equal the tender loving care bestowed by a good hedger on a hedge, but in an age when millions of unemployed hang about the corners of city streets and we don't have time to trim our hedges by hand, then the machine is better than nothing and, if it is the right machine, not too bad. Meanwhile the *smasher* hedge-cutter should be banned forthwith: anybody more sensitive than an ape can see that it is nothing but a murder machine.

If you did not trim your quick-thorn hedge at all, some of the little trees would flourish, others would be suppressed, and the ones that flourished would assume the natural form of the hawthorn tree and grow from ten to twenty feet high. They would look lovely like this – and flower every spring, which is a thing that the closely trimmed hedge does not do. But they would *not* keep out stock. There would be too much room between their trunks. All hedge trimming should be done in winter when the leaves are off the trees.

If a hedge does get out of control, there is nothing to do but *cut it right down*. It will then grow again and you will have a better chance of shaping it. I have seen this done very successfully in Suffolk by two men with a long double-handled cross-cut saw – the kind that were used for felling trees. The men stood each side of the hedge and simply sawed it down a few inches from the ground. Surprisingly, it worked. Traditionally the job is done by one man with a slasher, axe, and perhaps a bow saw too.

Now all the pundits and all the books will tell you that when you slash through a hedge branch or stem you should slash *upwards* and not downwards. The reason for this is that when you slash downwards you tend to shatter the bit of the stem which is left to go on growing; when you slash upwards you cut this clean. Also, in 'laying' a stem (which we shall discuss shortly) if you slash *downwards* (as in Sally's first picture) you leave a wound in which water can collect; if you slash *upwards* you don't. In Sally's second hedge-laying drawing the hedger has sawn the 'slovens' off to make the job look neater. The slovens are the bits of wood and bark that stick up after a downward slash.

Now I thoroughly agree with all the writers and pundits – it *is* better if you can slash upwards. But if you look at the average laid hedge (there are miles of beautifully laid hedges in Herefordshire, Breconshire and other Marcher counties), you will often see that this advice has been disregarded. The hedger has actually had to *do* it, not just write about it. Try cutting upwards when the beginning of your stroke (i.e. the ground) is only three inches from where you want to cut and you will see what I mean. It is far easier to slash downwards. In fact good old *Crataegus species* will put up with practically anything and come up laughing – and covered in sharp thorns just as before. So don't let the virtuous make you feel *too* guilty.

Hedge-laying is a delicious occupation and can be raised to a high art. It starts with the hedger, trimming or 'buck-heading' his hedge as usual, coming to a gap in the bottom part of a hedge where a sheep could get through. So he half slashes through a long fairly pliable branch next to the gap and bends this over to the horizontal, or nearly so, and winds the end of it into the hedge the other side of the gap. He has filled the gap, and the laid-over branch will go on growing, and put forth branches itself, and the gap is permanently filled.

But where a hedge has got right out of control, the hedger starts at one end and lays the whole hedge in the same manner methodically. He probably cuts a lot of surplus wood right out (and this can be used for dead-hedges elsewhere), he cuts straight posts to drive in there and then to help support his laid hedge, and he probably 'plashes' (weaves) along the top of these inserted posts, using hazel boughs from a nearby thicket.

He ends up with something like Sally's two illustrations, and this will be marvellously stock-proof, but will have to be done again in five or seven years. If you yearly slash the upward growth from the top of the hedge, it will last much longer, for it will be forced to grow more vigorously lower down.

A word about letting trees grow up in hedgerows. Nothing looks nicer, or is better for the birds; but do not forget that each side of every big tree in a hedge is a gap in the hedge, whether you like it or not. I find this perfectly acceptable, because you can easily fill these gaps with post-and-rail, or hurdles, or even horrid wire – and some of us have even seen this done with old Victorian bed-ends, brass knobs and all.

finished hedge with "heathering" on top
to finish it off

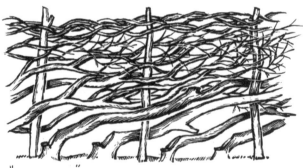

"slovens" sawn off for neatness

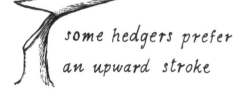

some hedgers prefer
an upward stroke

Now for various kinds of non-living fences.

Post and rail fencing

Fencing, of the kind that Abraham Lincoln used to split the rails for, is good-looking, stock-proof, non-damaging to such creatures as valuable horses, but damned expensive. It either has to be made of pressure-treated softwoods or heart of oak or chestnut. I was about to say this sort of stuff does not grow on trees. Well, yes, it does but it is still expensive.

Post and rail made from *sawn* timber is more expensive still. This generally has morticed joints, or at least housed joints. P and R made from round timber or, better, riven timber, may look more rustic but it will last longer. This will probably have neither morticed nor housed joints; instead the horizontals will be nailed on to the outside of the uprights with clenched galvanized nails. Strangely (but not when you think of it) this method is stronger and longer lasting. Cut-

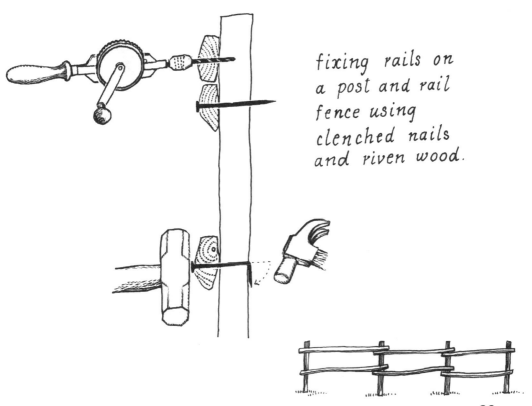

fixing rails on
a post and rail
fence using
clenched nails
and riven wood.

ting into the uprights for housed joints always weakens them, and it exposes end-grain for water to percolate into. And more surfaces are in contact, encouraging damp to linger. There is nothing stronger than a clenched six-inch nail. Before driving the nails, incidentally, you have to drill holes through the wood; otherwise you will split the wood or bend the nail, and certainly exacerbate your own temper. Then drive the nail, get a friend to hold a sledge hammer head against the head, bend over the point with a carpenter's hammer and hammer flat and well into the wood. This is as strong, in my opinion, as a bolt and nut, and much cheaper.

As for distances, the posts should be about four feet apart. The rails should be at a distance suitable for your stock: if you've got sheep and cattle you're not going to get away with less than five rails. Three is enough for just cattle and horses, particularly if they are fairly thick rails. Post and rail fencing is fine for millionaire race-horse breeders, or for fencing small pieces of land for poorer people. It is certainly not an economic way for a farmer to keep in stock.

And so we come down to wire. And at present, even with wire the price it is and soaring ever upwards, wire is what we generally do come down to.

Wire fencing

In what used to be called 'colonial' countries, such as Australia and South Africa, the **colonial** fence was evolved. This was affected by the high cost of materials, including white-ant-proof posts, and the fact that generally the land was flat and fences were long and straight. I learnt fencing in South Africa, where fences were measured in miles not yards. I tried to adapt the colonial fence to Pembrokeshire, where fields were tiny, field boundaries were twisted, boulders made driving in a post where you wanted it impossible and the land was anything but flat. It was a disaster.

The principle of the colonial fence was that you established enormously powerful anchors at the corners or ends of the fence, and thereafter every five hundred yards, you used 13½ gauge helical high-tensile steel wire, with a breaking strain of several tons, and you stressed it as tight as a violin string. The wire strainers we used

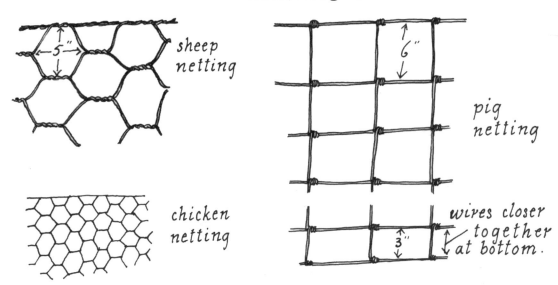

were capable of putting on a stress of two tons. If you snapped a five-hundred-yard length of wire at this tension it could come back and take your head off. Intermediate posts were planted at intervals of twenty yards. Such long intervals would be unthinkable using anything but the most highly strained high-tensile wire. 'Droppers', or small sticks, were wired on to the wires at intervals of four or five feet: they did not touch the ground.

In British conditions I would most highly recommend **wire netting,** well, but not excessively, strained and with posts every four feet. One or two strands of barbed wire should surmount it.

There are three sorts of netting in general. One is the light flimsy stuff used for chicken pens, rabbit hutches, and the like. This is useless for permanent fencing and would rust through in a few years. The other is what is generally called **sheep-netting,** which is shown in Sally's illustration. It is intended to be used for the movable fences that shepherds employ nowadays to confine sheep on turnips or other crops of arable land instead of the older, and much better, wooden hurdles. It stands rolling up well, is fairly light to carry, and does not need straining. It is not very suitable for permanent fencing. Lastly is what is often known as **pig-netting;** it is the best stuff to use for permanent sheep-proof fencing. It won't keep pigs in at all, unless protected by a well-strained length of barbed wire at or under ground-level; without this the pigs will put their cast-iron snouts under it and *lift*. And

Kinds of straining posts

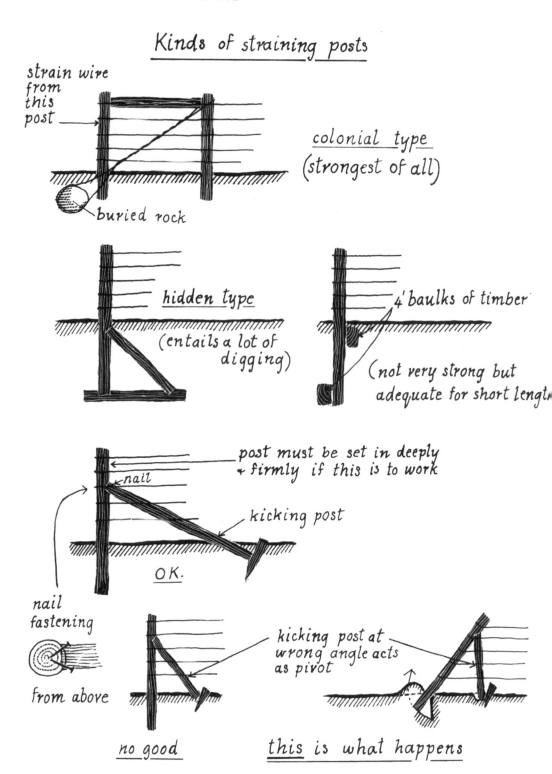

strain wire from this post

buried rock

colonial type (strongest of all)

hidden type

(entails a lot of digging)

4' baulks of timber

(not very strong but adequate for short length

post must be set in deeply + firmly if this is to work

nail

kicking post

OK.

nail fastening

from above

no good

kicking post at wrong angle acts as pivot

this is what happens

a pig can lift practically anything!

As can be seen from the illustration, pig-netting has vertical and horizontal wires. This means that it can be stressed sufficiently to keep it tight: polygonally meshed wire netting goes on stretching (and distorting) indefinitely.

A word about straining – or stressing – wire. Do *not* put undue strain upon it. If you do you do two things: take the spring out of it and crack the galvanizing, which lets it rust. Stress it just enough to put a little spring in it and leave it at that. And wire mesh needs stressing much less than single-strand wire, for obvious reasons.

I staple one end of the wire netting to a straining post, push a light steel bar through the meshes of the other end, and apply the wire strainer (or a block and tackle) to the steel bar. This pulls the mesh evenly. Staple to the intermediate posts, then tie on another roll of netting and pull that tight. It is no good stapling on wire *behind* the strainer of course – it won't be strained. It is best to hook the strainer to the fence further on, or to a tree, or other hold-fast, well back from the second straining post you are going to staple on to. It may be necessary to hammer the staples at the ends of the fence right home, so as to grip the wire. All intermediate staples just bang half in – don't bang them right in. Why? Because, firstly, you want the wire to be able to stress itself evenly right the length of the fence, secondly, as the years go by, you will wish to pull out rotten stakes and replace them. It is far easier then to remove the staples if they are not banged right home. And thirdly, when you bang a staple right home you damage the galvanizing of the wire and start it rusting the sooner.

If we take it that the pig-netting is three and a half feet in width and you strain two strands of barbed wire above it, each six inches apart, you have a four-and-a-half-foot fence, which is adequate for most things except deer. It is most desirable to have at least one strand of barbed wire; if you don't *everybody* climbs over your pig-netting, slackening and distorting it, horses will rub against it, and animals eventually learn to clamber over it. Barbed wire is your only true persuader – short of a thorn hedge.

As for end posts, corner posts, and any post to which you must strain wire, these should be impeccable. They must not budge an inch. Sally's illustrations show an assortment of designs. But it must be understood that an ordinary wire strainer, such as one buys at any agricultural ironmongers, will pull any but the best-made straining post right out of the ground. There is no substitute for the post held back by a stone or concrete anchor, (such as in Fig.1). Nothing will shift this. I know British practice favours the kicking-post but it is feeble in comparison.

Incidentally, it is important to notice that with pig-netting the meshes are bigger at one end of the span than at the other. OMCS will suggest that the *smaller* holes shall be at the bottom (to stop the smaller animals) but it is surprising how many people get this wrong, and suffer the consequent derision of their neighbours.

A pleasant, and quite effective, kind of fence is the **spile-and-wire** fence. This you can buy, very expensively. There is a charming factory in Faversham, Kent, where eager ladies *race* each other down a long room, working strange machines that make this fencing, while their companions place small bets on this or the other protaganist; but you *can* make this fence yourself, *in situ* too. You need soft wire (*not* high tensile): No. 14 SWG (standard wire gauge) is very good. I strongly recommend three pairs of wires – as with only two the spiles are more inclined to snap. The method of making is shown in the illustration. You just feed the spiles in and then winch the pairs of wires round with a steel rod (or the handle of a pair of pliers). Winch the opposite way between each two spiles. The spiles should be chestnut: there's not much point using anything else.

There are two methods of putting posts in the ground. All corner or end posts, straining posts, gate posts and other posts intended to take a strain have to be put into a hole already dug for them, a couple of inches bigger than they are, and either set in concrete or 'tamped' with earth. This **tamping** is often little understood. You do *not* tamp with a blunt instrument, but with a sharp one. You put a little dry earth into the hole around the post and tamp this hard with a heavy, pointed instrument. It is very hard work. After you have been right round you kick some more earth in and tamp some more. You go on doing this until you reach the top and the hole is filled. If you do it properly the tamped earth will be as hard as concrete. The

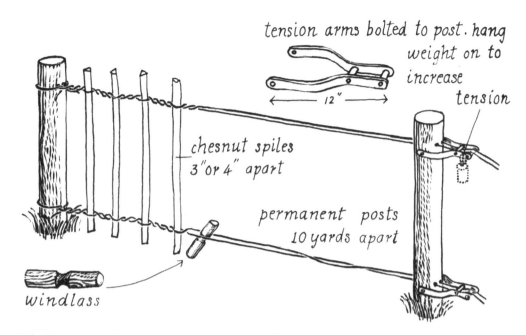

tension arms bolted to post. hang weight on to increase tension

← 12" →

chesnut spiles
3"or 4" apart

permanent posts
10 yards apart

windlass

Making a chesnut spile + wire fence.

reason why you use a sharp instrument for tamping is that then the force is taken by the earth *laterally* and not just downward. The earth is shoved sideways and not only downwards. Anyway, experience shows that a sharp tamping bar is far more effective than a blunt one and the heavier the better.

Lesser kinds of posts – the intermediate posts along a fence for example – can just be driven into the ground. But it is almost always better to use a steel bar to make a hole for them first. Knock 'em in with a rubber or wooden 'beetle' (maul or big hammer) and not a steel sledge which will invariably split them. If you split the top of a post you lessen its life considerably, for the water gets into it.

To creosote posts every three years or so is a good idea. Capping posts with metal to keep water from percolating down the grain is also beneficial.

Gates

Professionally made wooden gates are generally fitted together by housing the ends of the cross-pieces in mortices cut right through the uprights. This is a strong and good-looking construction, but it is laborious to do unless you have a morticing machine. Most country carpenters own one: it is a simple device, in which a strong chisel is set near the fulcrum of a lever. When you depress the lever the chisel is forced down into the wood and is driven right through it. Successive cuts form a mortice. You can do the same thing with a chisel and mallet – easier if you first make a series of holes along where your mortice is to be with a brace and bit.

Ideally a gate should be made of heart of oak. Professionally made gates always use sawn timber, but I seriously suggest making gates of riven wood. I have made scores like this, but of young ash, which is not going to last very long whatever happens. I have found fifteen years about the limit. Unfortunately I made all the gates on my Pembrokeshire farm about fifteen years ago! This is going to give somebody, very soon, an awful lot of work. If I could have made my

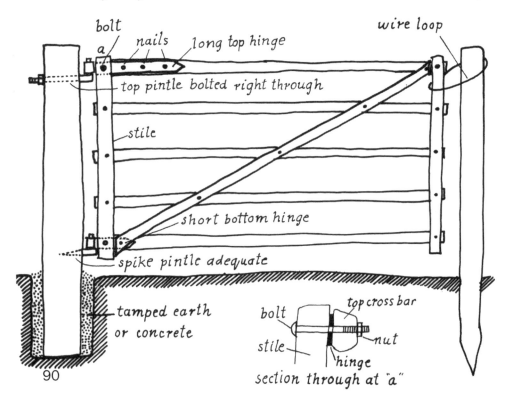

bolt   wire loop

a / nails   long top hinge

top pintle bolted right through

stile

short bottom hinge

spike pintle adequate

tamped earth or concrete

bolt

stile

top cross bar

nut

hinge

section through at "a"

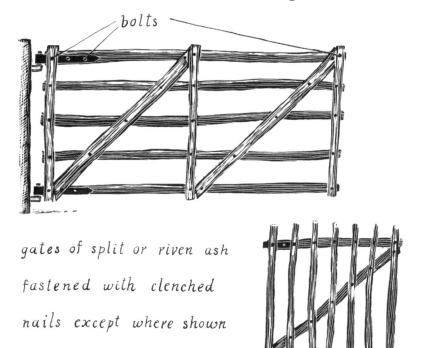

bolts

gates of split or riven ash
fastened with clenched
nails except where shown

gates of split chestnut or oak they would be good for another sixty years, but I had no chestnut on the farm and our sessile oaks do not have the straight clean stems needed for this sort of work. Probably the ash ones would have lasted far longer if they had been creosoted every three years. Alas, they were not.

To make a gate of riven wood you cannot use the morticing method, nor other housed joints. This may be an advantage, because observation shows that it is in the housed joints that rot starts first: moisture lingers there and eventually rots the wood. Instead joints are made by simply laying one member across the other and either bolting the two together or driving through and clenching a nail. I generally use small bolts for the three main fastenings and five- or six-inch nails for all the others. To tell the truth I believe that the clenched nails are nearly as strong as the bolts – and a darned sight cheaper. But, certainly at the hinge 'stile' (as the upright of a gate is called), bolts are justified, for at the top one bolt goes through two members (the stile and the top cross-bar), plus the top hinge, while the bottom bolt goes through three members (stile, bottom cross-bar, diagonal brace) and the hinge.

A moment's reflection will show that the *top* hinge is very important, for the whole weight of the gate (and any naughty children who happen to be swinging on it) is supported by that hinge. The top hinge must be long, and well fastened. The *bottom* hinge on the other hand is merely a compression hinge, not a tension one. Far from trying to pull it away from the gate post, the weight of the gate at the bottom is trying to push it into the gate post. The bottom hinge then can be quite short.

Now the design of gates. Whatever Sally's pictures show, a well designed gate should *always* have a diagonal stretching from the bottom of the hinge stile to the top of the latch stile as in Gate 1. It is not enough to have such a diagonal only halfway, as in Gate 2 as, in the ripeness of time, when other bits of the gate start to go, such a gate will inevitably fail on the top bar where the strut takes it – at 'c' on the drawing. Nor does the addition of a diagonal from 'c' to 'd' in Gate 3 help. Nor is the addition of a vertical, as in 4, very much better. And it is a mortal sin to have any gate (or door either) with the diagonal strut as in 5. A wooden strut should be a compression member, not a tension one. If you can imagine five fat small boys swinging on Gate 5, you realize that strut 'a' is then under tension. Strut 'a' in Gate 1 would be under compression and that is a far stronger posture. But to have two diagonals, as in 6 , is quite acceptable, and a strong construction. Strut 'b' in this gate takes no stress itself, but serves to hold the whole gate together. I have made a very long gate as in 7, and am told by an engineer friend that it is an acceptable construction. But for all gates not over twelve foot in length, type 1 is quite acceptable. Of course, all these gates will have minor cross-pieces nailed to them at a distance to suit the type of stock that you are trying to keep in or out. A five-bar gate of fairly generous timber will keep most things out, from lambs to horses.

When I cut down a tree for gate-making I first bark it and then measure off the longest length that I am going to need in the straightest and cleanest part of the trunk (ten-foot long gates are adequate for most honest purposes), and cross-cut (i.e. cut across the grain) this length out. I then rive (see chapter 6) as many pieces as I can get out of it of the sort of sizes I am going to need. I rive out the short pieces next, remember that I shall need a very good and stout straight piece for the hinge style, or upright. I then lay the gate out on the ground –

GATE DESIGNS

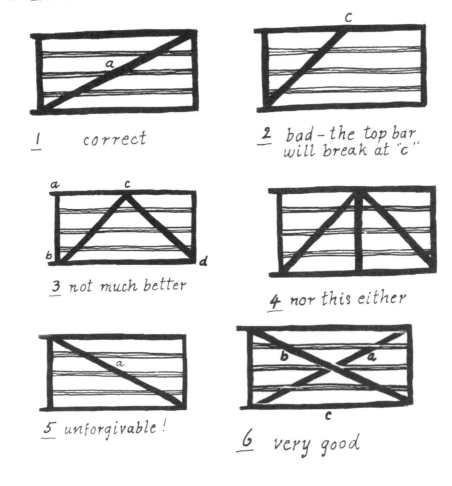

1 correct

2 bad – the top bar will break at "c"

3 not much better

4 nor this either

5 unforgivable!

6 very good

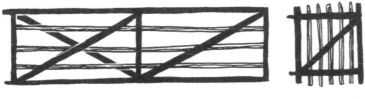

7 fine for a long gate

garden gate

starting to fa.

assembled b

togeth

long bits are trimmed off afterwards.

barking a post with a draw-knife

hanging finished gate.

not forgetting to include the hinges in the layout. Then, with a brace and bit for the bolt holes, and a small bit in a hand drill for the nail holes, I drill the appropriate holes. This may seem over-fussy, but I pour creosote or cuprinol in these holes – to prevent future rot. I then bolt and nail the gate together. No problem, anybody could do it – you don't have to be a carpenter.

If some of the members are not very straight it does not matter, although you will get a better looking gate if they are all pretty straight.

Now for **hanging** your gate.

The hinge post must be very firm and strong because, remember, it has to support the weight of all those fat small boys. (Don't tell me you can train small boys not to swing on gates – you *cannot*, no more than you can stop them playing in the hay barn.) So the hinge post must be a massive piece of heart of oak or chestnut, or a really hefty pressure-treated larch in the round, or an old railway sleeper in good condition. It must be either set in concrete or 'tamped' into its hole as we have described for fencing corner posts (see pages 88 and 89). The latch post need not be so strong but it must be fairly good too.

Now carry your gate to the hinge post, lay some bricks, stones, or

other supports on the ground in the gateway at the height you will want the bottom of the gate to be, stand the gate on these ('offer it up' as carpenters say) and wiggle it about until the hinges touch the hinge post. Use a level or plumb line to see they are vertical. Mark where they come with a pencil. Then remove the gate and drill holes to receive the stationary parts of the hinges with the brace and bit. It is most important that the *top* hinge shall be a bolt going right through the post with a washer and nut on it the other side. Remember, it carries the weight of the gate. The bottom hinge doesn't need anything like this: a simple spike driven into the gate post is sufficient (only drill a hole for it first or you may split the post). The weight of the gate is pushing that spike in – not tending to pull it out, and the more fat small boys there are swinging on the harder they push it in (and correspondingly the harder they tend to pull the top hinge out). The longer and heavier your gate of course (and small boys), the stronger you need your gate post – for it has to stand upright under great leverage and weight. Allow the wood to dry for six months then creosote or paint it.

There is no mystery about making gates in the way I have described. You do not have to be a carpenter or an expert. If you use the right wood, the gates should last half a lifetime. They look very good and the only thing you have to buy (if you have the trees) is a handful of nails, three small bolts, and two hinges. And it is surprising how often you can find these articles just lying about, salvage them from an old gate somewhere, or even off a rubbish dump.

A very short word on roads and paths

We quickly found in Burma during the last war that it was not wise to slant roads along hillsides as in Sally's drawing No 1. In a country where a rainfall of three or four inches a day was quite common, a road such as this quickly sheds its water over the side of the hill, or 'cud' as we used to call it. Unfortunately the road was apt to go with the water. So we learnt always to employ the configuration shown in drawing No. 2. This would last longer and, if we eventually got around to metalling the surface, indefinitely.

Even in countries with a rainfall of *less* than four hundred inches a year, it is better to use the second configuration. Even in England for example.

Paths can be anything from just a dirt path that you make naturally with your feet in a light-soil, well-drained garden, to a grassed path, which, if kept mown occasionally, is by far the nicest kind, to cinders chucked down every time you empty the ash-box of a coal-fired stove (if you burn *wood* you would never waste the ashes thus, but would use them as what they are: a high-grade fertilizer), to gravel, hardcore or asphalt, and concrete.

A gravel or hardcore path (hardcore is crushed stone of about 1" diameter) you can make yourself very easily – all you need is muscle, a shovel and a wheelbarrow. If you construct edges of brick, slate, stone or even board (the North Americans favour redwood for this purpose because it is cheap and lasts a long time in the ground. It is only cheap because the last of the redwood forest are being ruthlessly destroyed) and confine your aggregate between these (as in the drawing on page 98), you will have a tidy-looking and long-lasting path. But gravel and hardcore offer quite a lot of resistance to a wheelbarrow wheel. Also, weeds will grow through it. Asphalt or tarmacadam is ideal, but you have to hire men (generally gypsies) with the proper equipment to put it down. Concrete is very good for wheelbarrowing along, you can do it yourself, and it is very permanent.

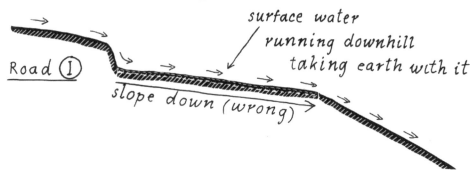

surface water
running downhill
taking earth with it

Road ①

slope down (wrong)

spoil from here could be used to build up outside edge of road
to form correct slope

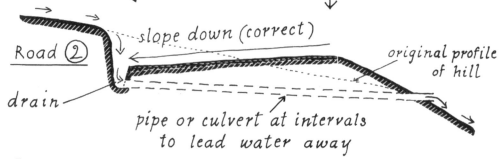

Road ②

slope down (correct)

original profile
of hill

drain

pipe or culvert at intervals
to lead water away

① will erode, ② will not erode

incorrect & correct sections through roads along steep slope.

If nothing heavier than you and your wheelbarrow are to go along it you do *not* need hardcore foundation, or a great thick concrete slab, or heavy wooden forms to pour into, or anything like it. If you roll out a roll of chicken wire (fairly fine mesh wire netting – the size of the mesh does not really matter) along the line of your path (don't be too fussy about levelling the ground first), put very light (1″ x 2″) strips of wood along the edges – you can either leave them there to rot or salvage them after the concrete has hardened – and then pour

section through gravel
or hardcore path.

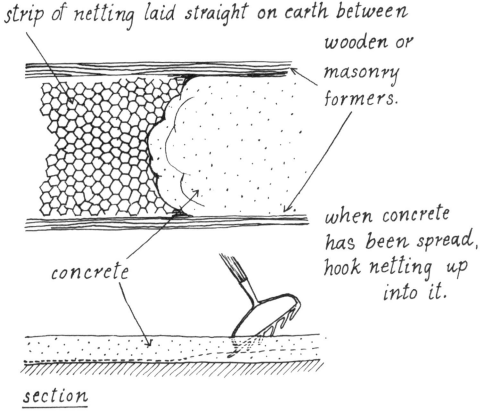

strip of netting laid straight on earth between wooden or masonry formers.

when concrete has been spread, hook netting up into it.

concrete

section

on a fairly rich mixture (say 1-2-3: one part of cement, two of sand, three of gravel), to a depth of 2½ inches, *lift* the wire netting an inch or two by poking a rake down through the concrete and hooking it, ram or tread the concrete well, you will have a perfectly adequate path. Don't blame me if it looks like – well, concrete. To make it look slightly better, brush the surface with a stiff broom before it sets. To make it look even less terrible, sow small pebbles (hens' eggs size or smaller) all over the wet concrete, press the pebbles well down into the concrete so they are out of sight (if the concrete has become too hard you may have to bang them in a bit with a wooden float), and let the concrete start to set. Now test it occasionally with a stiff broom and a hose. When it is still so soft that pebbles get dislodged, leave it alone. But when it becomes hard enough so that pebbles stay put, hose it well, at the same time brushing with the broom. The aim should be to have the tops of all the pebbles visible and yet have a pretty smooth surface for the wheelbarrow. The resulting path looks quite good and is pleasant to walk upon.

Chapter Five

Woodland

Before man arrived, most of the surface of Europe, and of North America in its eastern and far western parts, was covered with trees. The forests were of the type known to modern ecologists as 'climax forests': that is, they were a vegetation that had evolved as far as Nature would allow it, reached a balanced position, and then remained in the same state for millennia. Or at least that was the view currently held by most ecologists until recently: doubts are now beginning to arise as to whether there is such a thing as a climax vegetation at all; whether, in fact, change and development are not unceasing and ever will be. It can be argued that the Sahara Desert is an example of climax vegetation: an animal called man was evolved in it, or wandered into it, when it was in fact an enormous stretch of savanna forest; he domesticated goats, and with his cooking fires, and the other species with its rasping teeth and sharp hooves, destroyed the trees and reduced the land to its present state of 'climax vegetation'. And – who knows – maybe this same animal, man, hitherto so destructive, may have a change of heart which will make him reafforest the Sahara and turn it into a different kind of climax vegetation, one far more favourable to life on this planet. Who knows? It could be done.

Meanwhile man is, at the time of writing, at his peak of destructive inclination and powers, and so-called climax forests all over the world are being ruthlessly destroyed. The shifting sands of the Sahara are advancing over a front of thousands of miles at the appalling rate of thirty miles a year! The vast rain forests of the Amazon Basin will be completely gone, at the present rate of destruction, by the year 2005. This is being achieved, largely, by burning – often by dropping napalm bombs from the air. Thus all the carbon locked up in the trees is released into the air as carbon dioxide and already the chemical make-up of the air we breathe is being altered for the worse. Trees take carbon from the air in the form of carbon dioxide and release the free oxygen that we need to live, and there are becoming dangerously few trees left in the world. The same story – the denudation of the forests – can be told about every country and every continent. Everybody is now aware of the danger but nobody, apparently, can withstand the rapacity of the businessmen who are destroying the world's heritage for quick profits.

What all this means is that it is up to the enlightened landowner to plant trees above all else. Richard St Barbe Baker, the Founder of 'Men of the Trees', which is an organization responsible for the planting of millions of trees throughout the world, recommends that every land holding should have at least thirty per cent of its surface planted with trees.

It is a hard thing to ask of landowners that they should plant trees. Often the crop they plant will not come to maturity for a hundred years – sometimes longer. True, there will be a little profit from thinning, but that will not be for at least twelve years from the date of planting. There are, however, such things as food-bearing trees, and trees which have other products useful to man besides timber. Also, a surprising number of landowners have a conscience about this. I knew a timber merchant in Shropshire who had planted hundreds of acres of walnut trees right throughout Britain. Now these trees will only grow well on good land and they only come to maturity – and into profit – after three hundred and fifty years. I asked him why he did it, and he answered: 'Our ancestors planted walnuts for us – why shouldn't we plant them for our descendants?'

Well, if we *are* interested in our descendants (or if we are young and are interested in our old age) it is worth considering that trees increase in value at the same rate as money at compound interest – and are inflation-proof!

It is interesting to study the development of natural woodlands in the particular areas in which we live. There are unexpectedly few such native woodlands left in temperate parts of Europe or North America. In the North of course there are the vast coniferous forests, but these are being destroyed, chiefly for paper-making pulp, at an enormous rate and, in spite of attempts by governments in some countries to halt the destruction, it will not be many decades before there are very few of them left.

In temperate areas the killing-off of carnivorous animals, and the nurturing of herbivorous ones (such as sheep, cattle, horses and goats) means the natural regeneration of woodland rarely happens. Young trees, both broad-leaved and coniferous, are very vulnerable to grazing animals. Only last year I planted fifty young Scots Pines and every one was destroyed by a ewe and a lamb which got in from the road, in a couple of nights. Myxomatosis, the disease that *nearly* knocked out the rabbit, has enabled trees to grow where none could grow before; before that, the elimination of predators of the rabbit to favour game bird preservation had caused such a plague of rabbits that few tree seedlings ever survived unless planted in rabbit-roof-fenced land from which all rabbits had been eliminated. Although some rabbits survive every year, the disease is still operative, and perhaps the decades since myxomatosis have been the most favourable time for the natural regeneration of woodlands for centuries.

I fenced off five acres of land on my farm in Pembrokeshire against farm animals fifteen years ago. It is good heavy land, fairly free of water. The climate is mild and wet. The ground soon got covered with gorse and bracken, the gorse gradually winning from the bracken, and then, after about five years, I noticed thousands of young birch beginning to grow through. Among these was a sprinkling of alder, in the wetter parts, and ash in the drier. In one of two places there were young sessile oaks. The area is now an impenetrable thicket of mostly birch about fifteen to twenty feet high. In places we have thinned the birch and there young oak saplings are growing. I have no doubt that in the parts left to Nature, some of the birch will be crowded or shaded out, some trees will reach maturity, and then, when a mature birch dies, young ash or oak will establish themselves in the space it leaves, and I shall be surprised, if I am still alive, if in fifty years time the area is not predominantly ash and oak – chiefly oak – and that this will become the 'climax forest'. But I fear only my ghost will be there to enjoy the scene.

On sandy land, gravel or heathland, birch and rowan (mountain ash) will probably predominate, with Scots Pine in the northern countries. On the chalklands of southern England, northern France and other temperate climates, the beech is generally the dominant wild tree, but, where the soil overlying the chalk is deep enough, oak, ash, hazel, box, and sometimes yew and juniper will be found. On the dour limestones of northern England ash, oak, sycamore and maple are likely to be found. On wetlands everywhere the alder will be the dominant tree, with various kinds of willow intermingled. Poplar will also grow in such places if it gets a chance, but will probably have been planted.

Planters of trees should consider the trees that naturally grow well on their soil and in their climate. Planting oak on heathland is a very unprofitable exercise, and planting birch on good fertile loam is a terrible waste, for such land could be used for growing more valuable species, such as sweet chestnut, oak and ash.

To plant any trees, on any soil, provided they have hope of survival, is better than nothing. But if we are going to the trouble of planting trees, it is surely desirable to plant the right tree in the right place.

One of the most important things to remember when planting a tree is that no matter how tiny a seedling is, it will grow very *large*. One of the factors that caused me to migrate from Suffolk to Pembrokeshire was the fact that the little conifer plantation at the end of my garden, on the south side of it, grew to such a height that my best piece of land and my house were completely shaded. The plantation was not mine and therefore I could not cut it down. It is said that when Mahomet couldn't get a mountain to move to him, he moved to the mountain. Well, when I couldn't get the Corsican Pines to move away from me, I moved away from the Corsican Pines.

Many a person has planted a screen of nice little trees in his country garden, or on a piece of land near his house, only to find the little dears growing into giants that cast too much shade, take up too much land, and indeed, sometimes by the action of their roots even cause his house to fall down. Of course you can always cut a tree down, but if you do you are left with a stump, which can be a beastly nuisance and cause labour and expense to take out. We will discuss this problem in the 'Cutting timber' section of the next chapter.

So plan your planting well before you start it. Consider what the trees will be like when they are fully grown. Consider which kinds of trees you want and what you want them for. Consider the part each tree will play in the ecology of the piece of land of which you are trustee. Remember, for example, that native species – particularly species that have been native to your country for a very long time – will attract and nurture far more wild life than exotics. This is because many species of insects, birds and fungi have evolved over the millennia to live symbiotically, or parasitically, with native trees. Exotic species had such symbiotic relations with the species of their native countries but do not have them with the wild creatures inhabiting the country to which they are strangers. Thus the oak, alder, ash and rowan, in Britain, will be found to support far more other forms of life – birds and insects for example – than imported trees such as the sycamore.

This is not an argument for not having any exotic species at all. Personally I love the sycamore and I love many exotic conifers too. But it is a plea for always having a good proportion of natives sprinkled among the exotics.

A word must be said here about monoculture: the growing of only one species. In my submission it is never a good thing. Nature never practises it: left to herself she clothes the ground with many species and peoples the forests with a multitude of different kinds of animals. The result of this profusion is that disease organisms cannot run through an area like a forest fire and therefore seldom get out of hand. The odd individual here and there will succumb to disease, but this is natural, indeed desirable, for none of us is meant to live for ever.

Also, one species will have different demands on the minerals of the soil than another and – by its leaf-fall – put back into the soil elements needed by other species: thus each kind of tree and plant thrives in association with other kinds. Very little is known about this subject of 'companion planting' yet and very little research has been done on it. Some woodlands, in temperate climates, can claim to have existed before the last Ice Age; where woodlands have existed for many millennia, as in the tropical rain forests, a vast concourse of different species of trees and plants is found, and in animals too: in the Amazon forest two thousand species of birds have been counted. All forms of life in such forests are dependant on other forms of life, and attempts to grow tropical rain forest trees in isolation have generally proved unavailing. But the *biomass* of such diverse forests is enormous: they have life abounding.

Let us therefore learn from Nature and make our plantings diverse. The practice of the Forestry Commission , in Britain, and of its equivalent in many another country, of planting huge stands of trees of one species, is dictated by reasons of economy: it takes much more labour and skill to manage forests of mixed species and mixed ages – so-called 'sustainable forestry', or, as it is sometimes called, 'selection forestry' – than it does one-age, one-species forests. But selection forestry, when skilfully carried out, yields more timber per acre over the centuries, is far less liable to fire damage, and to damage from pests and diseases. It is only a matter of time before parasites and diseases evolve that will sweep through the huge one-species forests and do great damage; in fact this is already beginning to happen. And selection forestry is much better for the soil.

There are two other factors in favour of mixed-species, mixed-age planting. One is that such plantations are richer in wild life. Go into any of the Forestry Commission's one-species plantings, and see how many birds, or other animals, you see. I'll warrant it won't be many. Go into a mixed-age, mixed-species woodland – particularly one with a high proportion of broad-leaved trees – and you will be half deafened by the song of birds! The other advantage is that the latter kind of woodland looks much nicer. It is beautiful. Nothing, except possibly a sailing ship or a pretty girl, is more beautiful than a mixed deciduous forest.

Even the Forestry Commission, which only does what it is told by the government and does it extremely well and professionally, has begun to yield to public opinion to the extent of planting 'amenity belts' of deciduous trees round its huge masses of spruce or pine forests; it has even, in a few cases, indulged in planting hardwood or broad-leaved trees.

But we who have small areas of land to plant can go in for mixed planting to our hearts' desire, for we will be able to devote the skill, judgement and loving care to the job that makes for success.

I must here consider two ancient and still excellent methods of tree culture: coppicing (and 'coppice-with-standards') and pollarding.

If you cut most hardwood trees down to the ground, new stems will spring up very quickly from the stumps. This is called **coppicing.** Now these stems can be cut off, or harvested, at frequent intervals – from seven years to about fifteen years depending upon what kind of material you want. Of course this is never 'saw timber' – the poles you cut will only be a few inches across, but they can make excellent fence posts, bean poles, hop poles, and, above all, firewood. It is much the quickest and most productive way of growing firewood. And you can cut thus again and again: the root systems will last at least a hundred years with this treatment, and sometimes longer.

Pollarding is doing exactly the same thing – but, instead of cutting down at ground level, you cut above the reach of grazing animals. Again, you can use practically any hardwood tree. Thus, once your trees are of a sufficient size that their main trunks defy the teeth of herbivores, you can grow them for many decades with animals grazing underneath them. Meanwhile we all know the pollarded willows along the slow-flowing rivers of eastern and southern England. The shoots were harvested from these every year or so for basket-making

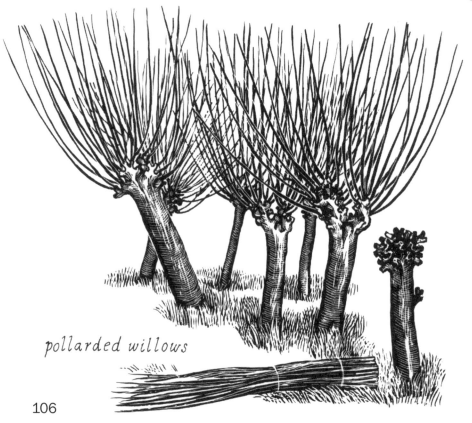

pollarded willows

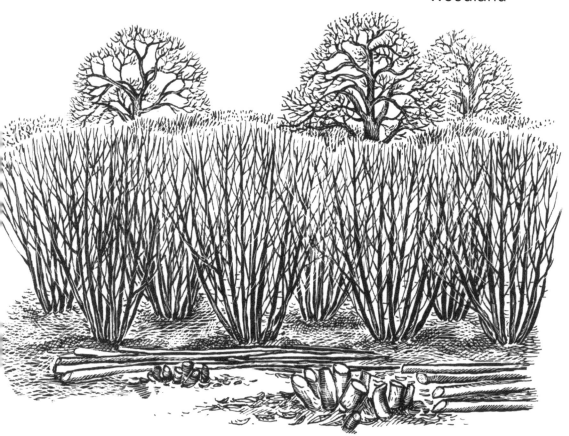

A coppice of sweet chesnut.
with standards in the background & cut stools in the fore.

and hurdle-making, and will be again when plastic gets more expensive.

Coppice-with-standards is an excellent old practice, out of fashion now but due for a revival. It generally consisted of sweet chestnut and/or ash coppice wood, with the occasional mature tree – often oak growing up over it. The disadvantage from the modern forester's angle is that the 'standards', as the trees left to grow big are called, are not forced to grow tall and straight by the proximity of other trees. The advantage in days of yore was that very disadvantage: the oak trees left grew many crooked branches. These were essential for the 'crooks' needed for the building of wooden ships. Naturally grown crooked branches formed the knees and other bent members of a ship's construction.

In any case, coppice wood is no longer in high demand. The hop yards have shrunk, fields are bigger and therefore do not require so much fencing material, and many other uses of coppice wood no longer apply. But, as we shall discuss in our section on firewood, coppice and pollard wood will be needed more and more in future.

The trees most suitable for coppicing are: sweet chestnut (the best of all), ash, hornbeam, hazel, oak and birch. Hornbeam and birch will not endure long under this regime. We will discuss which trees do best on which soil, and what timber is best for which purpose, in due course. All broad-leaved trees will coppice, but not all are so suitable for it as the trees I have mentioned. At present there is limited use for hazel coppice material – although it's always nice to have a few nuts! All pollarding and coppicing should take place in winter, when the trees are dormant.

I will not discuss one-species one-age plantations except to repeat that I disapprove of them.

Mixed-species one-age woods are another matter, for first plantings on bare soil, but after the first fellings have been extracted then underplanting should proceed in the spaces left.

Trees can be divided very roughly into two groups from the point of view of the forester: 'shade-bearers' and 'light-demanders'. Shade bearers are those trees that can tolerate growing in shade. Light-demanders are the opposite. It is a good idea to mix the two. The reasons for this are that the shade-bearers on the whole improve the soil while the light-demanders do not; on the other hand, the light-demanders tend to be the more valuable timber. Nothing builds up the soil better than a stand of beech trees, while the more valuable oak, grown pure in a wood, will impoverish it. Difficulties can (and do) arise with mixed planting when one species grows faster than another and blankets it out. If the slower species is a shade-bearer this may not be fatal. But with skilful planting, and a knowledge of what grows fast and what more slowly, this disadvantage can be minimized.

It can be seen from all this that it is easier for a huge landowner such as the Forestry Commission to decide to blanket a whole area with the same species than to plant mixed woodlands, where the choice of mixture involves considering the soil, the aspect of slopes, and so on. Mixed planting requires skill, which is in very short supply. But the blanket one-species planting can be compared to factory farming. It is cheap to do and therefore profitable, but it by no means makes best use of the land, nor produces the finest timber, and above all it leads to ugly results and is bad for the soil. After all – if *we* don't care what our country looks like, who the hell will? Good mixed forestry can be achieved by small landowners, who have the time to give the tender loving care that this sort of forestry requires. What old Fritz Schumacher called the *TLC factor*.

The Earl of Bradford, on his Tavistock Woodland Estate in Devon, has perfected a system ('the Bradford continuous-cover system') which has proved eminently workable and economic. His Lordship grows chiefly Southern Beech (*Nothofagus procera* and *Nothofagus dombeyi*) mixed with various softwoods such as Western Red Cedar, Western Hemlock, Californian Redwood. In case any reader disposes of enough woodland to cause him to be interested in the system, I will describe it as I understand it. I have been to Tavy Valley to look at these woodlands and can vouch for it that they look productive, healthy and beautiful; although I could wish that the proportion of the broad-leaved Nothofagus species trees was higher in relation to the conifers. As the Southern Beech trees apparently grow as fast as the conifers and are much better timber, I can see no reason why more are not planted.

The land is divided into main sections each 20 yards by 20 yards. Each section is sub-divided into nine sub-sections 20 feet by 20 feet. Cutting of existing woodland and subsequent planting and thinning is so arranged that after 54 years *one* of the sub-sections in each main section has a mature tree on it. (That is, it is not a full-grown tree after that time, but it is nevertheless suitable for cutting for timber, and has lived through its fastest-growing period.) This tree is cut out. By then its crown will have almost filled its sub-section of 20 feet by 20 feet. If there happen to be naturally grown seedlings under it, these are left, to be thinned when of thinnable age, but one is always left to grow to its own 54 years. Every six years the forester enters the main section and fells one mature tree in one of the sub-sections. Thinning goes on wherever needed. Thus each main section yields one 54 year old tree every six years, and 54 years after the first mature tree is felled in the first sub-section there is another mature tree there to be felled in its turn. Thus the cycle goes round and round and it can be seen that – once the system is established – there will be trees in every main section of every age up to 54 years old, and of as many species as the forester likes to introduce. Of course if there are no suitable self-sown candidates in a sub-section after the mature tree has been felled, then the forester plants some, in the usual way. And care should be taken that a tree of a different species to the one that has just been felled should be left to grow to maturity the next time. In this way there is a proper rotation of crops, so that the same old species is not using up the same elements from the soil as the previous crop did.

It can be seen from the above description that this kind of forestry calls for intelligence, knowledge and sympathy, and it would be very difficult to get unskilled labourers to carry it out over vast acreages. One does not have to stick to the trees that Lord Bradford plants, but it is obviously important to choose shade-bearing trees because, when they are first planted, they have to bear a lot of shade. We will consider which trees are in this category in due course. One great advantage, of course, is that the young trees have the protection of their taller neighbours in other sub-sections, and therefore do not suffer the wind and frost damage suffered by trees planted after clear-felling practices.

I hope I have not frightened to death any beginner tree-planters by this description of a rather complicated, if eminently sensible and quite logical, tree management plan. The owner of a small area of woodland, who does most of the work himself, or at least closely supervises it, can be completely flexible and relaxed about the whole thing. He can merely act as a benevolent influence in the forest, taking out trees when they are mature or about to deteriorate, cutting out bad specimens, thinning where needed, brashing (cutting off the lower branches) – to reduce fire risk, improve access and produce knot-free timber – and planting young trees anywhere that natural regeneration has not been adequate. In his replanting he can introduce new and experimental species. Provided he leaves a good proportion of native species, I see no reason why he should not try any exotics that he fancies: the Southern Beech is turning out to be a *marvellous* tree, but more of that anon.

Chapter Six

Trees

Here are some rather bald facts about the various requirements of the species of trees most likely to prove valuable in Northern Europe:

Trees which will grow well at a high latitude (i.e. in the North): Scots Pine, larch (particularly Japanese), spruce, Wych Elm, birch.

Trees that prefer the south of England or even warmer latitudes: oak, common elm, ash, beech, Sweet Chestnut, Austrian and Corsican Pine, walnut, eucalyptus.

Trees that will thrive at over a thousand feet: Sitka Spruce, spruce, Japanese Larch, sycamore, birch, Corsican Pine (I have seen fairish beech at 800 feet).

Aspect: (whether north-facing or south-facing) is important in hilly country. Surprisingly there is often less late spring frost damage on north-facing slopes than on south-facing ones. Why? Because on south-facing slopes trees are lured to put out their buds too early by the treacherous warmth, and then get 'em nipped off by a May or June frost. A further consideration is that south slopes tend to dry out faster – north ones remain moist. And also south- and west-facing slopes suffer stronger winds.

Trees best suited to south- and west-facing slopes: Austrian and Corsican Pines, oak, elm, chestnut (by this I will always mean 'Sweet' or 'Spanish' Chestnut *Castanea species* and *never* the Horse Chestnut *Aesculus species*), maple, sycamore, False Acacia.

Trees best suited to northern and eastern slopes: ash, beech, larch, Douglas Fir, Silver Fir, hornbeam, spruce.

The above does not mean that the trees *have got to be* planted on slopes with the aspects described: simply that, other things being equal, they tend to do better on them.

Trees that make good shelter belts against strong winds: spruce, Austrian Pine, Corsican Pine, *Cupressus macrocarpa*, beech, sycamore, Sitka Spruce (a very rapid grower but likes a wet climate).

Light-demanders: larch, Scots Pine, poplar, willow, False Acacia, Corsican Pine, oak, ash, chestnut, elm, alder, Austrian Pine, locust, plane, walnut, Wayfaring Tree, Sea Buckthorn, big tree.

Moderate shade-bearers: lime, maple, sycamore, hazel, Douglas Fir, spruce, Sitka, birch, redwood, Horse Chestnut, Swamp Cyprus, all rose family trees.

Good shade-bearers: beech, Nothofagus, hornbeam, Red Cedar, Silver Fir, hemlock, sequoia, evergreen oak species, holly, box, most spruces, yew.

Trees that will grow near the coast subject to salt winds: elm, Evergreen Oak (*not* other oaks), tamarisk, Sea Buckthorn, escallonia, and, of softwoods, Sitka Spruce, Lodgerpole Pine, Austrian Pine, Maritime Pine, Stone Pine, Monterey Pine, Monterey Cyprus. Corsican Pine is less resistant as are oak and Scots Pine.

Trees that will stand city air pollution: most broad-leaved trees but *not* evergreen ones. No evergreen trees can stand up to city smoke. The reason for this is that they hang on to their leaves or needles too long and the stomata, or pores, get blocked up. Of course the city tree *par excellence* is the plane, but ash is good, so is lime, willow, poplar, rose family trees and maidenhair tree. Beech does not thrive in polluted air.

Exacting trees or trees that need good soil: oak, ash, chestnut, sycamore, elm.

Moderately exacting trees: larch, spruce, lime, hornbeam, beech.

Accommodating trees or trees which will put up with poor soil: Scots, Corsican and Austrian Pines, birch, Japanese Larch, red cedar.

Trees best for firewood: hardwoods, and of these ash, birch, oak, holly, beech, hornbeam, maple, sycamore, locust, lime, plane and all the rose family trees are best. Ash and holly are special in that they will burn really well even when freshly cut: all the others must be seasoned, if cut while alive; preferably for at least nine months. Willow is not bad if really dry and alder, *faute de mieux*, but it must be dry too. Personally I burn tons of it.

Chestnut, alas, is a poor firewood. Pity, as it is so good in every other way. If I were to plant trees just for firewood I would (and do) plant ash and oak, and coppice them. Birch is good if very dry – it makes a very hot fire. The Norwegians have a saying that if a house catches on fire, a birch log did it. But then, besides birch, all they have got is beggarly softwoods.

Of softwoods it can be said that they will all burn, but only burn well when seasoned and *kept in the dry* – for after they are seasoned they absorb water like blotting paper. Everyone who has been to Switzerland or Austria must have seen the huge stacks of sawn and split logs up against the walls of the chalets – all with covers of some sort over them to keep the rain and snow off. Burning any wood (except, I repeat, holly and ash) unseasoned is a thankless business, for most of the energy in the wood goes to drying it, and not to warming you or cooking your dinner; also a large amount of tar and other gunge forms in your chimney from wet wood. All softwoods spit like hell. This does not matter in Continental enclosed stoves – let 'em spit away, they can't do any harm. Enclosed stoves are becoming more common in Britain now and softwood, well seasoned, is fine for them. I am burning a lot of Scots Pine and larch on an open fire at the moment, and I just let it spit and be damned.

Trees best for durability: of hardwoods (which are best anyway): heart of oak, heart of chestnut, locust, walnut, Tulip tree, False Acacia. Of softwoods, the true cedars and the true cypruses, larch (pretty good), Californian redwood and big tree, Douglas Fir and yew are all not bad but *much* better if allowed to dry out well first and then creosoted or otherwise chemically treated, at least if they are going to be set in the ground. Ash, birch, alder, elm, hornbeam, and spruce wood are hopeless in the ground.

Trees for under-water use: elm pipes (hollowed-out logs) are still extant and usable from Roman times. Elm is very durable if kept under *all* the time. Alder, though much softer, is also durable under water. Both these timbers will survive out of water if kept always dry: neither can stand wet-and-dry conditions.

Box is your hardest and heaviest English wood. It is frequently used for *priests*: the small truncheons that are used for dispatching salmon. (The name comes from the fact that the implement gives the salmon its last rites.) Hornbeam is also hard and was much used for gear teeth and other machinery parts before steel came into better supply. The various rose family woods (apple, pear, plum, etc.) were also used for such purposes.

Soil improving trees: beech is by far the best soil improving tree; others include *Nothofagus species*, or the Southern Beech, and 'hornbeam'; Silver Fir, the spruces and Douglas Fir are all great soil improvers, for they have a heavy drop of leaves or needles which increases the humus content of the soil. The various pines improve the soil for the first thirty years or so; after that thinning, and the opening out of the trees, exposes the soil to the sky too much and fertility tends to get leached out and the soil to deteriorate. Oak, ash, birch, poplar, elm and larch will not improve the soil – in fact they will harm it if they are grown pure. When all these trees are young and close together they at least protect the soil; when they get older they have to be thinned, they open out, they don't have a heavy enough leaf fall, and the soil deteriorates.

The above may seem of academic interest only to the owner of a large garden or very small estate, although to somebody intending to plant up an acre or more with trees it is not academic at all. For anybody with land, it is most important to know how to improve the soil, what trees grow well together and why. In the next section we will consider tree planting, the care of trees, the qualities of different species, the uses of their timber, and how to harvest and convert the produce of the woods.

The qualities of the commoner trees of temperate climates

HARDWOODS

Alder *(Alnus glutinosa)*. Grows like a weed in wet places, particularly along streams. Being infested with it myself, I cannot imagine anybody planting it, but people do. Useless as posts – it rots very quickly in the ground, but it can be used, if treated against woodworm first, for interior rough constructional use; the round, barked poles can be used for supporting thatched roofs or even corrugated iron. Grows fairly straight and coppices freely. Has root nodules in which bacteria fix nitrogen: a useful attribute, as it thus helps enrich the soil. Was used for clog soles. When really dry makes an indifferent firewood. Good for charcoal.

Alder Buckthorn *(Rhamnus frangula)*. Grows wild, often with alder. Never grows very large. Wood used to be used for making charcoal, which was used for gunpowder (hence its German name: *Pulverholz*).

Ash *(Fraxinus excelsior)*.Does very well on calcareous soils, but grows in most places, including very wet ones. Is light-demanding and, to reach large sizes, needs good soil. A very valuable timber crop – it can reach a hundred feet, with a fine, straight, clean stem when grown in the right conditions. For timber it is never planted alone: it is often planted together with larch, or it is grown as the standards in coppice-with-standards. It is a fine tree for coppicing itself, producing quickly large amounts of most useful material: the best firewood there is and good cleaving wood. No good in contact with the ground, but wherever toughness and resilience are required, ash is used. Hocky sticks, oars, framing for vehicles, or even for aeroplanes, were generally ash. One of the most valuable timber crops to plant on good land (particularly overlying chalk or lime). Comes into leaf late and therefore not considered very ornamental.

Beech *(Fagus sylvatica)*. A magnificent tree and will grow to a hundred feet in a hundred years, with much greater girth than the ash tree. Superb wood for turnery, for the grain is even, it turns or carves well,

ASH

and does not split or 'move' once seasoned. Much used for furniture – it bends well under steaming. Good for dairy utensils and draining boards. An extreme shade-bearer, can be planted under other trees and it will catch them up. A great soil-improver. Doesn't coppice well – throws up very crooked shoots which are, though, good for firewood. Will grow on most good, well-drained soils, but likes calcareous ones best. Not frost-hardy when young, though I have seen beech quite high in the Welsh Mountains, but in such places it needs a nurse crop like pine. Fine tree for underplanting other species.

Southern Beech (*Nothofagus species*). The distribution of various forms of life about this planet is a never failing source of wonder; it seems marvellous to me that right down on the Antarctic tip of South America grow a number of species of beech very similar to our European beeches. The Southern Beech is much faster growing, and bids fair, one day, to be the hardwood tree planted commercially in Northern Europe above all others. Lord Bradford has established a large plantation of it, and Bradford Estates, Tavistock, Devon, is the best source of planting material. I saw some specimens at Kennedy Park, in County Wexford, the other day that were planted just twelve years ago and are now biggish trees; at least twice as high and with twice the girth that one would have expected. They like the same sort of soil that the European Beech likes, yield the same sort of timber. *N. procera* seems to be the preferred species to plant in the British climate.

Birch (*Betula pubescens and species*). Grows further north than any other tree in the world and will stand extremely low temperatures. Is found at about three thousand feet high in Wales and Scotland. Is not fussy about soil (thrives on gravels and sands) but is very light-demanding. Not much good for coppicing, as the stools quickly die out; its timber is of little value, though a good firewood if allowed to become really dry and on poor soil worth growing for that use alone. A good nurse crop for more valuable species and very ornamental: Coleridge called it 'the lady of the woods'. Its wood can be used for turning into such things as bobbins, bowls, brush backs and such things. You can tap birch trees in spring for the sap, which flows copiously, and can be made into wine. Rots very quickly if driven into the ground – I think it even beats alder in this respect.

BEECH

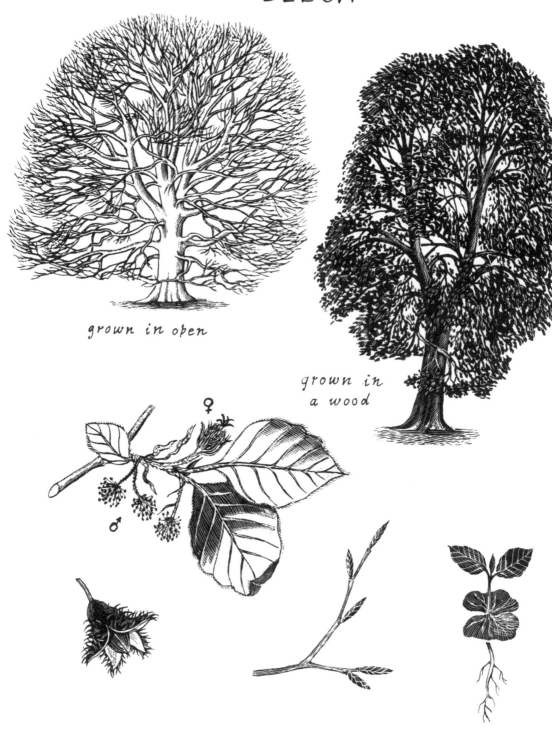

grown in open

grown in
a wood

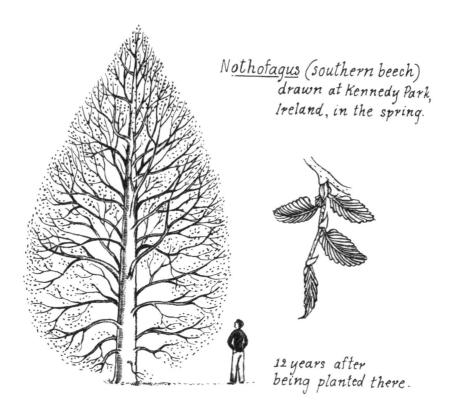

Nothofagus (southern beech) drawn at Kennedy Park, Ireland, in the spring.

12 years after being planted there.

Chestnut (*Castanea species*). Not to be confused with Horse Chestnut – a completely different tree. It is sometimes called 'sweet' or 'Spanish chestnut'. It is far simpler just to call it by its name.

For my money by far the best tree for a smallholder or small farmer to plant. The trunks grow straight and true, at least when grown in a plantation, the timber is most excellent – the heart is at least as good as heart of oak and there is a lot of heart to sap wood. It is the riving wood *par excellence*, it lasts for decades as posts driven into the ground, it grows quickly and, withal, when it gets mature in a warm climate will give you a harvest of the most excellent nuts. Not a good firewood though. In France it is a notable producer of pig and cattle food. It is the best of all coppicing trees, but will grow to heights of 110 feet and huge girths if left alone. Far far more of it should be planted. It does not stand intense cold – is best planted on south or west-facing slopes in Britain and at not too great altitude. It stands shade when young but not when older. As coppice, it improves the soil but *not* as forest tree and should not be grown in pure stands for this reason.

SWEET CHESTNUT

Elm *(Ulmus species).* Surprisingly, a close relative of the nettle – and the hairs on the small leaves of the English elm tend to be irritant. There are many varieties, but the tree species: Common or English Elm *(U. Procera),* Rough-leaved Wych Elm *(U. glabra)* and Smooth-leaved Wych Elm *(U. nitens)* are the most important ones. The English Elm was the best timber, until it was practically wiped out by Dutch Elm Disease. It is significant that this tree, which seldom seeds, was entirely diffused from suckers, and thus every English Elm in Britain was probably a clone of one tree. Asexual reproduction has its dangers and it is not surprising that eventually a disease arose that wiped what was in fact an extended individual out. The too-successful fungoid parasite, and the too-successful beetle that carried it, by killing the elms, have wiped *themselves* out, so maybe it would be sensible to plant English Elms once again.

Elms like good, rich, deep soil, well drained but well watered. They became so conspicuous in hedgerows in fertile counties because this position suited them. They are only moderately shade-resistant. They are very wind-firm. The Wych Elms put up with worse soil than the English Elm and their timber is as good.

The wood will not split and is thus useless for riving, but very good for chopping blocks, butchers' tables, and so on. It does not make good firewood. Elm wood is beautifully marked and deserves better than just to be used for coffins. The tree is quick-growing. It is one of the best underwater woods and is used for keels of ships and other underwater uses. It is fine for turning. The great horizontal branches are rather apt to snap off without warning and land on top of the heads of picnickers.

Hazel *(Corylus avellana).* This friendly and useful little tree was grown widely in southern England as coppice for hurdles, wattles for wattle-and-daub building, thatching spars, and other such uses. Large acreages were grown, the little trees being planted in groups of two or three and about ten feet apart, cut right down the second or third year, which made them coppice (throw out many shoots), then cut down every seven to ten years, when the wands were the right size to produce goods. Before the wire fence was invented, hazel hurdles were essential for making and mending fences, and for folding sheep over turnips. In days of hay and corn ricks, thatchers used thousands

hazel twig
with nuts.

of spars (the split hazel rods driven into the thatch to hold it down) and – particularly in the chalk areas of the country where brick-earth was scarce – split hazel rods made the framework on which the mud daub of wattle-and-daub buildings was made. We see plenty of Tudor – and pre-Tudor – houses in which the wattles under the mud daub are still as hard and good as new. Hazel coppice is very productive and – if the various industrial building materials ever become scarce – will become worth its weight in gold, for excellent houses can be built of timber-frame, hazel, mud and thatch alone.

And, as for the nuts, they are very nice to eat. Pack the unshelled nuts in dry salt and they will last for ever and taste delicious when you finally shell them and eat them.

A suggestion that I keep meaning to try but never have: what about grafting improved Kentish Cob Nut scions on all those straggly hazel bushes growing in your woods?

Hazel is very hardy, will grow on most soils, and very shade-resistant.

Holly (*Illex aquifolium*). Good for ornamental hedges, but won't keep stock out. The wood, though small, is hard and good to work, can double for box, be turned or carved, and if dyed black looks like ebony. Its best use is for Christmas decorations – but only the female tree bears berries. A great shade-bearer. Won't grow well near cities, being an evergreen.

Hornbeam *(Carpinus betulus).* Looks like a beech, but is more closely related to the hazel. Was once much grown as a pollarded tree for firewood (Epping Forest is full of trees which were, in the past, treated like this); the point of pollarding is that the growing points are kept up out of the reach of browsing cattle: coppiced trees would suffer. Most excellent firewood. No good for driving into the ground, but it is perhaps the hardest of British woods and was traditionally used for vice screws, pulley sheaves, gear teeth, mallet and maul heads, and could well be again. It'll blunten a chisel or a plane like nobody's business.

Horse Chestnut *(Aesculus hippocastanum).* Surely every sizable piece of land ought to have one Horse Chestnut – just for the little boys? Also of course for the superb flowers, and the general luxuriance of the tree. It grows so fast its timber is not much good for anything except a little cabinet work. It must be planted right out in the open: no good in a wood or as a hedge tree.

Laburnum *(Laburnum anagyroides).* Very beautiful: the German name *Goldregen,* or 'Golden Rain', describes it well. It makes its own nitrogen, being a member of that privileged family the *Leguminosae,* but its pods are poisonous (besides being copious). I know places in Wales where it grows freely in hedgerows and nothing seems to get poisoned, though, so I shouldn't worry about it too much.

Lime *(Tilia species).* Fine foliage makes it ornamental, and flowers have a sweet scent and can be used as a tisane. Timber no good out of doors, a poor firewood, but fine for wood carving as the grain is fine, soft, and even. Piano keys are made of it.

Locust *(Robinia pseudoacacia).* Sometimes called 'Robinia' after the French botanist who described it when it came from America. It is also leguminous and therefore very good for poor soils: it will even grow on slag heaps, and if I had one I should plant this tree over it. Poor old Cobbett was much maligned because he imported sacks of seed from America and sold them to English landowners saying that this was the tree to end all trees in usefulness. The landowners failed to make a fortune out of it and wanting to beat Cobbett anyway for his radicalism, used this as a stick to beat him with. Actually it is a very useful little tree (besides being ornamental), because it is quick growing, the wood is very hard, makes fine fence posts and it is a fine firewood.

Maple *(Acer species)*. The Field Maple *(A. Campestre)* is nice to see growing as a bush or scrubby tree in hedgerows, but I can't imagine anybody wanting to plant it. Norway Maple *(A. platanoides)* is an ornamental tree which leafs out early in spring and looks spectacular in the autumn. Some of the Japanese maples are ornamental too.

Oaks *(Quercus species)*. The English oaks are the Sessile *(Q. petraea)* and the Pedunculate *(Q. robur)*. They are the commonest hardwood trees in Britain and their demise would leave a far bigger hole in our landscape than that of the English Elm, which makes it all the more astounding that the government will not stop the importation of American oakwood which is quite certain, sooner or later, to introduce the American oak disease.

The oak should be planted, cultivated and nurtured in Europe and North America more than any other tree. It is the tree of history, the tree of tradition, and above all the tree of the English-speaking peoples. Heart of oak is as good as heart of chestnut for fence and gate posts, the branches and off-cuts make the finest firewood (seasoned – it's stubborn stuff to burn green), oak cleaves well, is often *hewn* with adze and side-axe into squared beams – the sap-wood being taken off – and can be sawn into planks, beams, or anything else you want. It may be only of academic interest in this age of plastic dustbins used for brewing beer, but barrel staves are made of riven oak. To do this you cross-cut your tree to the lengths required, rive into quarters, rive off the sap-wood *and* the heart of the tree, then rive the staves out along the radii of the tree. Oak rives very well in this direction owing to the well developed medullary rays (rays running from the centre of the tree outwards) of the tree. Now it is important that there should be one of these medullary rays in each barrel stave, because it is these that make the stave water- and alcohol-proof. Most barrel staves nowadays come (when they come at all) from Eastern

OAK

Europe and Russia. It is only laziness that stops us from growing and making our own.

Oak will only grow well on good land (the best is good enough for it). It is not considered 'profitable' to grow it any longer, but we of this plastic generation would have regretted it if our ancestors had thought the same. Oak should not be grown alone to maturity; when the crowns of the trees open out, as they do after, say fifty or sixty years, the oak should be underplanted with beech to cover and improve the soil. Oak is not a soil improver. In any case it should never be planted as a pure crop: nature abhors monoculture.

Oak is considered mature, on good land, at 120 to 130 years but can be left another century or two if needed. The longer it lives the more heart wood there will be in proportion to the sap-wood, which is practically valueless. Nobody knows how long oak will survive: after a few centuries they cease to make visible rings: but a thousand years is pretty certain. The cultivation of such trees as the oak and the walnut requires the state of mind that can only be found in long-enduring land-owning families. Now these are nearly extinct, it is important that some other motivation should be found to make people plant these enduring trees: it has been shown that state-owned forestry organizations certainly have not.

Evergreen Oaks, such as the **Holm Oak** *(Quercus ilex)*, are only grown in Northern Europe for ornamental purposes, although their timber is hard and good for furniture making. They do not, in northern climates however, grow timber fast enough to make them a worthwhile commercial tree. It is good firewood.

Turkey Oak *(Quercus cerris)* grows quickly but its timber is not very durable and it is said to be very bad firewood. The various **American Red Oaks** produce good timber and look beautiful while they are growing. They are often planted on the borders of plantations for 'amenity' reasons.

Sycamore or Great Maple *(A. Pseudoplatanus) is* much maligned nowadays by people who say, quite rightly, that it is a 'foreign' tree and therefore a tree which does not support a great diversity of living things on it as, for example, does the oak. Well of course all trees

SYCAMORE

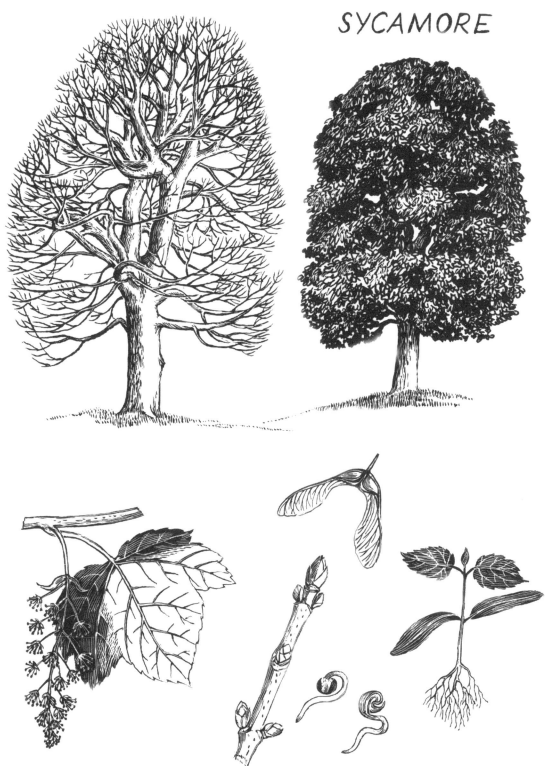

in the British Isles – with the possible exception of the Dwarf Birch – are foreign trees because our islands were covered with ice not very long ago and the only trees here are trees that either managed to move across the land bridge with the Continent, before the sea broke through this, or have been brought here by birds or man. A mature sycamore is a magnificent tree: I have one quite near my Welsh farmhouse and it is a constant source of satisfaction to me. Already there is a reaction setting in against plastic and the time is coming when the clean, white, even–grained wood of sycamore is going to be in demand again for turning, draining boards, kitchen utensils, and so on. It makes good furniture, too, and the wood will take stains well. It is easy to plant, easy to grow, is not fussy as to soil or climate. It stands city pollution well, doesn't mind sea breezes, will grow on builder's rubble even. For my money a very good tree to plant. And what if it does seed very freely so you get hundreds of tiny seedlings growing under every big tree? A swipe with the hoe is all that is needed to cure that imagined ill. But maybe the fact that I have a son-in-law who is a wood turner makes me think especially kindly toward this tree. Good firewood, but wood not durable out of doors.

Plane (*Platanus acerifolia*). Although, as its specific name suggests, its leaves look like the sycamore, it isn't of the same family. Being the most resistant tree of all to city smogs and fogs, it is much planted in cities. It is withal a magnificent-looking tree and grows to a great size. Its wood is good for furniture-making. It has well developed medullary rays and its timber is known as 'lace wood' to the furniture trade. It stands up to heavy and continuous pruning very well and is thus kept small in city streets.

Poplar (*Populus species*). The Lombardy Poplar (*P. nigra* variety *italica*) is what makes us think of van Gogh's paintings (or those of other Low Country artists) whenever we see mile-long avenues of these trees along straight French or Belgian roads. It is a fine tree to plant if you want a strong vertical accent among other foliage. It is much used as a screen for hiding such things as factories and aeroplane hangars, but, as it sheds its leaves in winter, it is only partially successful for this. Unlike some other poplars, it is safe to plant it near buildings.

The so-called Black Poplar (there are scores of poplar hybrids), if planted on clay soil, should never be allowed near buildings; many people say that a hundred feet is the minimum distance. This is because it takes so much water out of the soil that the soil dries out, cracks and eventually may undermine foundations. People will tell you to plant poplars and willows on badly drained land to dry it out. It is true that they dry it out in the summer time, when it is dry anyway, but of course they don't in winter becase they're dormant, which is when you really want to dry it. Black Italian Poplar is an extremely fast growing tree on good, well-watered land. It is very profitable to grow in such situations, being used for making matches, chipboards and other such uses.

The Trembling Poplars (White, Grey and Aspen) look beautiful. I have a small bunch of Aspens in the most remote part of my Pembrokeshire farm – God knows how they got there, for they are miles from any others of their kind. They die back and rot before they get very tall, but seed freely. The Balsam Poplars have delightfully scented sticky buds and it's worth planting one for the smell alone.

To grow poplars commercially (and these will probably be Black Italian), rear them from cuttings, cut these down to the bottom-most bud at a year old, leave for another two years and then plant out at twenty foot intervals. They won't do well on bad land or in a frost pocket.

Walnut *(Juglans regia).* It is a disgrace that more walnut trees are not being planted. Our generation reaps the benefit of the plantings of more generous generations in the past, but we almost wholly fail to consider our posterity. It takes a hundred years to produce a worthwhile tree, for it is only the heart wood that is valuable, and walnuts may be left to grow on profitably for three centuries; all this time, after the first score of years, the trees are paying a good rent with the most delicious nuts there are. Every big garden should have at least one walnut tree in it and walnuts should be planted in groups here and there in mixed plantations. They want good, dry, loamish soil, plenty of light, and plenty of space. The heart wood is some of the finest hard, high-quality, beautifully figured timber there is. During the Napoleonic Wars the walnuts of England were slaughtered to provide the stocks for Brown Bess – the English musket that broke the French cavalry charges at Waterloo. It is still used for fine gun stocks. The nuts are an important food source in France, but in Britain the tree does not crop every year.

Willow (*Salix species*). Like the poplar, the willow is endlessly hybridized, and thus generally grown from cuttings. If you have very good, well-drained but yet well-watered land, Cricket Bat Willow (*S. Alba Coerulea*) is a profitable tree to grow, as it fetches very high prices after only twenty years. Beware *water-mark disease* though, which spoils it for this market.

Osiers are generally *S. viminalis* and are planted on a large scale on goodish moist land in low-lying situations for basket material. The withies are cut down nearly to the ground and thereafter cut every year for baskets, hurdles, basket chairs and all the rest of it. Because of floods of cheap and nasty basketry from the Far East, this industry is in severe decline. I stuck in a couple of score of withies in a piece of rocky wasteland in Pembrokeshire about ten years ago and allowed them to grow to pollard size. Every year we cut their whiskers and reap a great harvest of withies which we fail to use – although my wife used to make 'Moses baskets' out of them for friends when they had babies and sometimes somebody does get around to making a basket.

A touch on basket-making. If you cut the withes before the end of September, you can strip the bark off them with bare hands. This is what gypsies do and one of them taught me the trick. Cut much later than that it is hard to bark them: you have to do it as per the illustration. If you store them *in* water, they are supple enough to work. If not, boil or steam them. If you boil them with the bark *on* and then bark them you get them pleasantly stained brown. Basket-making is very easy as you can see from the illustrations.

tool for taking the bark off withies.

forked blade, sharpened inside edge

Other willows (such as Crack and White) grow quite large and make a fine white very light splinter-proof timber. They should be planted far apart on wet alluvial ground and they will grow to eighty feet very quickly.

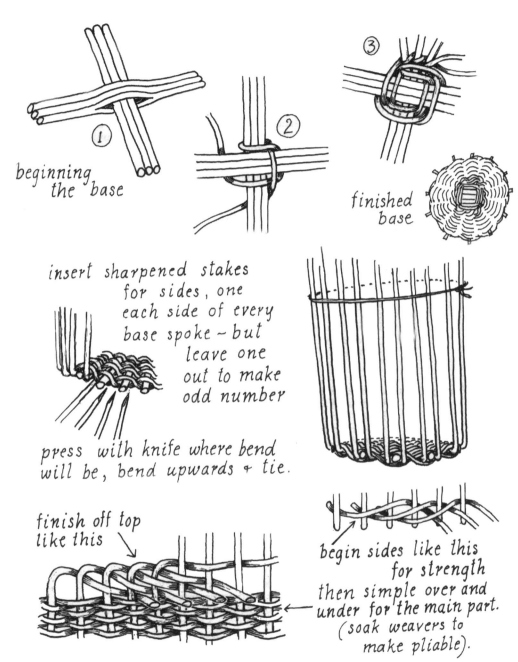

① beginning the base

②

③ finished base

insert sharpened stakes for sides, one each side of every base spoke ~ but leave one out to make odd number

press with knife where bend will be, bend upwards + tie.

finish off top like this ↘

begin sides like this for strength then simple over and under for the main part. (soak weavers to make pliable).

Stages in making a simple basket

131

The Goat Willow *(S. Caprea)*, which grows like a weed on my farm, is good for practically nothing but to act as a nurse crop occasionally to frost-tender trees such as Sitka Spruce. I use tons and tons of it for firewood, after drying it for a year, and it is not as bad for that purpose as the books will tell you it is but not very good either. It is nice to see it growing naturally in wild, wet places but for anybody to *plant* it would be as sensible as planting thistles.

I have a wild wet ten-acre wood in Wales, which is chiefly alder and Goat Willow, growing as high as these trees will grow. But there are a few big old mother ash trees and thus thousands of young ash seedlings growing under the alder and willow. These, not being shade-bearers, grow weak and straggly and fight towards the light and eventually, alas, die out. But if, as I do, you go in with the axe or chain saw and fell a proportion of the old trees so as to let the light in, up rise the ash and make fine trees.

Establishing trees

All trees can be grown from seed – although some very seldom are: the Common Elm, for example, seldom sets seed in England and was (prior to Dutch Elm Disease) nearly always multiplied from suckers. The various willows seldom breed true from seed and are multiplied by cuttings. It is unlikely that the small landowner will bother to grow trees from seed. Oak grow very freely from acorns and a very positive thing to do is to walk about with a pocketful of acorns and just pop the odd one into the ground along hedgerows or in bare places in woods. Conifers are very hard to grow from seed and are far better bought as small trees from a nursery. Apart from oak, hardwood trees are better sown in the nursery where they can be carefully looked after. Generally the seed is sown thinly in rows in a seed-bed, in soil enriched by leaf mould or compost, carefully shaded from too much sun, sheltered from wind, protected from weeds and pests, and 'pricked out', or transplanted into a holding bed, after two years, and then, after another year or two, planted out into its final planting site. To sow seed where it is going to grow to maturity is a dicey business, as it is very hard to nurture and protect it outside of the controlled conditions of the nursery. Therefore it is almost always an economy to buy your trees from a nursery.

the Author's wild wet woods with self-sown ash saplings
under mainly alder + willow

If it be a good nursery the seedlings will have been pricked out at least once, and this first transplanting will have caused them to grow fine bushy roots that will make them grow the better when you transplant them yet a second or third time. Nurserymen talk of small trees being 'two-year-two' or 'two-year-one', and so on. This means, in the case of 'two-year two', two years in the seed-bed and two years in the holding bed. Thus a two-year-two tree is four years old. At that age it stands a very good chance of survival when you plant it out. Three winters ago I went into my wild wet woods in Pembrokeshire and brutally pulled a thousand young ash trees out by the roots. I didn't even bother to dig 'em out – I just pulled 'em out. I transplanted them, very roughly, in a wet boggy boulder-strewn patch where little else would grow. Amazingly nearly all of them have taken, although many of them must have been six or seven years old and were very long and leggy. Most other species would not have tolerated this treatment. Trees are best transplanted young. There are, however, two ways of making it possible to plant trees at a more advanced age. One is to transplant them several times when they are very young. Every time you transplant them you force them to put out a bushier root system and you prevent them from putting too much effort into driving down a deep tap-root that will be difficult to keep intact and transplant. The other method is by root pruning. You dig a trench around the growing tree and sever its wide spreading roots (you must also undercut it to sever any tap-root); this forces it to concentrate on the bushy mass of fine roots that will enable it to survive late transplanting. Trees nowadays are transplanted by these methods at as old an age as twenty years. Great care has to be taken, however, in doing this, to keep a ball of soil around the roots by tying hessian or sacking around, very gently easing the tree out of the ground, and as gently transplanting it. The roots must then be kept well watered for some time if the weather is dry.

But three- or four-year-old trees will transplant pretty easily. Such trees may be one or two feet high. If you have only a few trees to plant, it is better to retain balls of soil about their roots, but it is perfectly alright, and much quicker, to plant them with bare roots.

The best way to carry them from the nursery is in one of those horrible plastic bags which litter our countryside nowadays, and it is a good idea to throw a handful of water in with them before tying the neck of the bag. It is most important to stop the roots from drying out – this is what kills trees, as people find out every year, year after year, when they try to transplant the Christmas tree that has been suffering in their overheated living room for at least thirteen days.

The safest manner of planting is called 'pit planting'. Before you take the little tree out of its moist plastic bag, dig a pit which is a little deeper and wider than the spread of roots of the tree. I always loosen the soil in the bottom of the pit too, for the depth of a spade, and, if I have some and it is a very special tree, chuck some compost in. If you intend to stake the tree, and all trees do better staked, now is the time to drive the stake into the bottom of the pit. Not after you have planted the tree, in which case you will tear some of the roots with your stake. You only really need a stake in an exposed position; in forestry planting nobody ever bothers about stakes.

Take the little tree out of its bag, place it very gently in the pit, then sift the soil gently into the roots, with some compost if you have some; pull the trunk up and down a little to get the soil well mixed with the roots, making sure there are no air cavities; the soil must be in close and intimate contact with the roots. See that the tree is at about the same depth in the ground as it was before. As you get more soil on top of the roots stamp on it. Many people are afraid to stamp too hard for fear of tearing the roots. Do not be too afraid. Over-hard stamping is better than under-hard. When I have finished filling the pit with earth, I do a positive devil's dance around it. Thump the soil well down. Then, if you have water, water. Tie the young tree to the stake but do not, as I once did, tie the little tree tightly with corlene string, which does not rot or give. I killed several young larch like this when I was young and even more ignorant than I am now. You can buy tree ties from a nursery, make something up yourself, or don't stake the tree at all.

Now if you have lots of trees to plant you cannot go to all the above rigmarole, and if they are small seedlings you will not need to. The best way then is 'notch planting'. Drive your spade into the ground one way, then drive it at right angles to cut a 'T' (some people favour an 'L'). At the junction of the two slits lift the turf, or surface of the ground, put your baby tree into it, pull it up an inch or two to make sure the roots are straightened out, let the earth fall back on the tree-

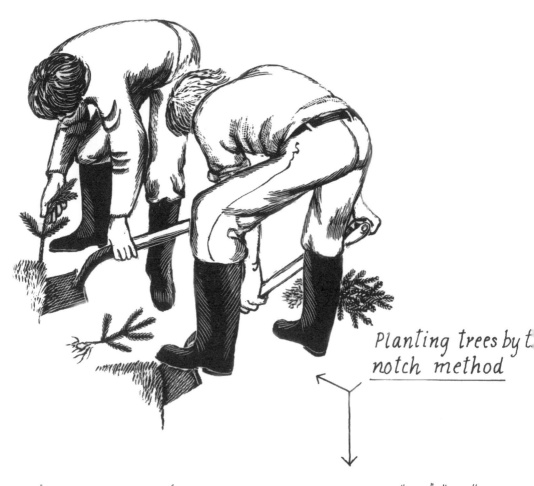

Planting trees by the
notch method

turf cut through in a "T" or "V" shape,
prised up, & small trees inserted at "a".

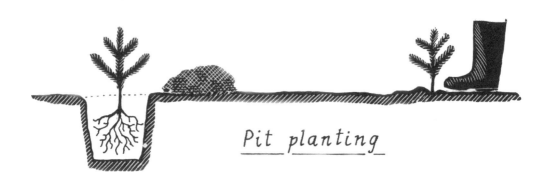

Pit planting

and *stamp hard*. This sounds very casual and slap-happy but those hundreds of thousands of acres of conifers that blanket our hills were planted just like this.

On peat lands, the method used is to cut out a square of turf with a spade, invert it on some uncut turf, and plant the tree in a slit in the inverted turf.

As for the **spacing,** or distance apart that trees should be planted, it depends what you want. If you are growing trees for timber production plant them close together (from 4 to 6 foot apart). The idea of this is that as the trees grow they will crowd each other and draw each other up to the sky. The trunks will thus be tall and straight. Further, they will shade and thus suppress each others' side branches. Then the forester goes in, maybe every 7-12 years and **thins.**

Thinning should be done little and often, and the nice thing about it is that the thinnings are generally either useful or worth some money. Light-demanding trees should be thinned for the first time after about fifteen years; shade-bearers five years older than this. After the first thinning, subsequent ones should be made about every five years for light-demanders, eight years for shade-bearers. Little and often is the rule. Thinning is, like so many other things in husbandry, common sense. Cut out all twisted, damaged and dead trees, cut out trees which have been so suppressed by bigger trees that they will not do very well, cut out 'wolf' trees, as big, vigorous twisting trees are called, cut out some of any obviously overcrowded trees. The trees *should* be crowded, but not too crowded. Better to thin lightly at the first thinning and then harder as the years go by to leave the trees that are to form the final crop room to grow. Make sure the ground is kept covered by a canopy: it should never see the sky. Of course if you are going to *underplant* after thinning, then you must thin very drastically. But with any wood you might well start out with two thousand trees per acre and end up with two hundred a hundred years later, but these will be giants.

What many good foresters do is to plant a pure stand of oak, larch, or ash, and wait until the tops are beginning to thin out. You will know when this is happening because a growth of coarse undergrowth will begin to grow between the trees. With larch this will probably begin to happen in about fifteen years; with oak in thirty or forty. This is the time to make a heavy thinning of the trees (cutting out perhaps three quarters) and then underplant with a shade-bearer and soil improver, such as beech. Western hemlock or red cedar are sometimes used for this purpose too: better still a mixture of all three. The shade-bearers will grow up quickly between the first crop, shade out the weeds beneath, and, by their shade, kill off the lower branches of the first (more valuable) crop and thus make for cleaner and straighter timber.

As to the initial planting space: quick-growing trees, such as larch, Douglas Fir, ash, chestnut, *Nothofagus,* Red Cedar and Sitka Spruce, should be planted about five foot six apart; slower species perhaps four foot six inches. To find how many young trees you will need per acre, divide the number 43,560 by the product of multiplying the distance between rows and the distance between plants in the rows. This gives you number of trees per acre. Thus if you plant in rows four feet apart and the trees are four foot in the rows you will multiply:

4 x 4 = 16
43,560 divided by 16 = 2,722 trees per acre.
Of course when young trees are planted, anywhere, they should be kept as free as possible of weeds or they will be smothered.

In case the time scales involved in sylviculture are putting you off, I would tell you that when my youngest daughter was born, twelve

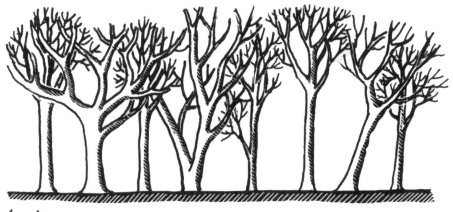

before

years ago, I planted about a quarter of an acre of mixed larch, chestnut, Norway Spruce, with a sprinkling of geans (wild cherries), sycamore and one or two other odds and ends. The trees were only a foot or two tall when I planted them. The thinning of the Norway were sold, as the years went by, as Christmas trees, only a few being now left. The rest could do with thinning now, but from time to time I have cut out larch which were overshadowing my chestnuts. Many of the trees are well above the roofs of the farm buildings now: they form an impenetrable screen to the gaze of passers by, a complete windbreak from that direction, and a most marvellous place to creep away and meditate in (or go to sleep for that matter), for nobody has ever yet discovered me in there! And the twelve years have slid by extraordinarily quickly! But I am indifferent to whether I shall see the benefit of planting trees with my corporeal eyes. I shall go on planting trees, I hope, until the year that I die.

Cutting trees down

The standard way to cut down any tree except a simply enormous one is this. First, with axe and hand saw trim off any awkward buttresses at the base of the tree with the axe. Don't do any unnecessary trimming though – OMCS (Old Mother Common Sense) must be consulted at all times. Felling trees is hard work and don't do anything for nothing. Then 'put a sink' or 'cut a bird-mouth' with the axe into the side of the tree towards which you wish the tree to fall. The bottom of the 'sink' or 'bird-mouth', which is just a wedge-shaped

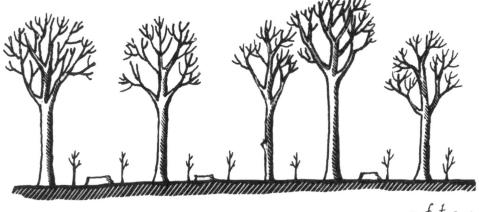

after

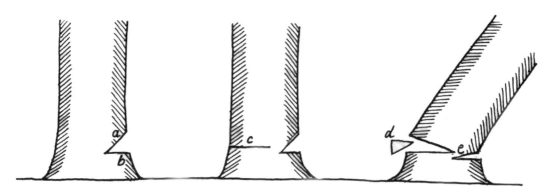

Felling a tree.

cut out sink or birdsmouth on side tree is to fall. making 1st cut at "a" and 2nd at "b". Next make cut "c" on opposite side above base of sink. If saw jams with weight of tree use wedge "d" - continue sawing until tree bends over "hinge" "e" and falls.

cleft, should be horizontal – the 'roof' of it slanting. The cleft should go about a third of the way into the tree.

Then put the saw into the other side of the tree, horizontally, just an inch or two above the apex of your bird-mouth. Saw away until either the tree falls down or, as generally happens, the weight of the tree settles down on the saw and stops you sawing. If so, drive in wedges at the back of the saw cut. This helps in three ways: it takes the weight off your saw, it stretches the fibres in front of the saw and makes them easier to cut and eventually, if you bang the wedges in from time to time, pushes the tree over.

With a chain saw the process is *very* much quicker. You cut the bird-mouth with the chain saw, then attack the back of the tree with it too, again, slightly above the bird-mouth. You should really use hard rubber wedges with a chain saw, because of the danger of touching a steel one with the blade.

The chain saw is probably the most *dangerous* tool anybody is likely to use in the countryside. It will cut through the hardest wood very quickly and if it touches human flesh the result can be nasty. If you use one of these tools you must think carefully all the time what you

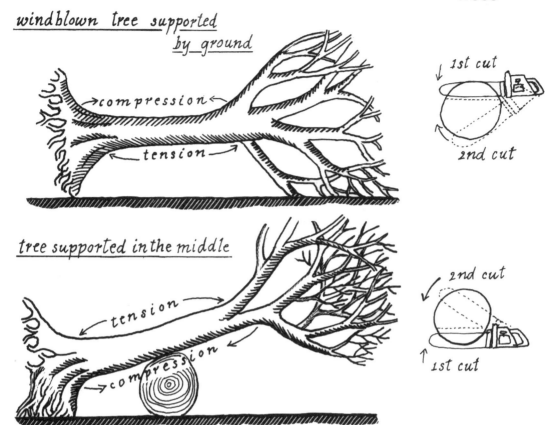

windblown tree supported by ground

compression

tension

1st cut

2nd cut

tree supported in the middle

tension

compression

2nd cut

1st cut

are doing: be on your guard and always anticipate accidents, such as you slipping, the tree kicking back or the chain swinging round your leg. Do not work with a chain saw if you are tired. Wear ear-pads, a hard hat, heavy gloves, armoured boots.

When I cut down trees in my woods, I find that as the trees are severed, they tend to lodge on standing trees. I then have to fell the standing trees to get them down. Sometimes half a dozen tallish trees will come crashing down, very unexpectedly, around my ears and there I stand, knee-deep in mud, caught up with brambles, and with a juddering chain saw in my hands. It is not a pretty situation and don't get in such situations unless you know what you are doing and have had a lot of experience. Remember – the tree you are cutting can always *kick back* – sometimes with no warning. The kick can kill you. Wind-fallen timber is very dangerous. Any wood under tension is dangerous; when you start to saw it, it can practically explode. Saw as close to the butt (root end) of wind-fallen timber as you can, saw on the compression side first, but withdraw the saw before it gets pinched; then saw the tension side and look out! If the tree seems very dangerous, relieve the tension by making shallow cuts all along the tension side first. OMCS will tell you that a tree supported horizontally at each end will be under tension along its bottom side; one supported in the middle only will be under tension along its top side. And always, before you start to fell a tree, make sure you have a clear escape route.

A word about cutting limbs off standing trees. Cut the branch off as near the main trunk as you can – don't leave untidy stumps. But if you try to cut down from the top of the branch at first (which will be under tension from the weight of the branch) the branch will split and the split may run far down the trunk. If you try, however, to cut upwards from below, the compression will jam your saw. Instead, make a shallow cut from below first but stop before the saw gets jammed, then cut from the top but several feet away from the trunk. Lop the branch right off there. Then, with very much lessened tension, cut down next to the trunk. You will then not split the tree. Cut limbs off trees in winter when the leaves are off the trees and these are dormant.

A hint about lopping branches off a felled tree. Start on the bottom ones (the ones nearest the ground as the tree lies recumbent). Then work up to the top ones. Why! Because if you start with the top ones they will fall down on top of the bottom ones and make the latter

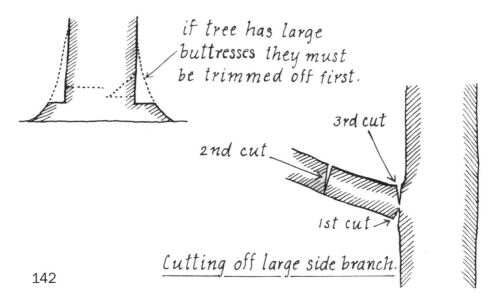

if tree has large buttresses they must be trimmed off first.

3rd cut

2nd cut

1st cut

Cutting off large side branch.

hard to get at. It is *far* better, when felling trees, to take Mrs Beeton's advice and 'clear as you go'. Fell a tree, lop it, drag the slash (amputated branches) out of the way and pile them tidily, deal with the trunk and get it out of the way, then fell the next tree. When working single-handed I have found myself completely surrounded with a mass of fallen trees and have to cut my way out to the open. Working like this is extremely dangerous – you cannot get out of the way if the unexpected happens, which it is inclined to do. As an A. A. Milne character pointed out, accidents don't happen until they happen. And, with a chain saw, when they happen, they happen. It is far more sensible to have somebody with you when felling trees in the woods. A good chain sawyer can keep two good men busy just clearing up after him. This enables him to concentrate on the job he is doing.

If a tree is leaning and you want to make it fall at right angles to its lean you can often give it quite a tilt in the right direction by the way you cut it. Take out the sink, or bird-mouth, on the downhill side – the side in which the tree is leaning. Then start your felling cut not quite opposite this sink but at an angle and away from the direction in which you wish the tree to fall. For some reason or other this gives the tree quite a twist in the right direction.

To pull a leaning tree backwards against its lean is more difficult than many people think. A rope from the top of the tree to a holdfast in the direction in which you wish the tree to fall is not much help: as soon as the tree is felled, it will swing sideways – at right angles

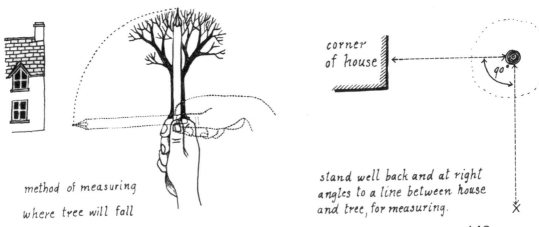

method of measuring
where tree will fall

corner of house

stand well back and at right angles to a line between house and tree, for measuring.

to the rope – not in the direction in which you thought the rope was pulling. The rope was *not* pulling of course – it was merely tight. Even a winch will not always pull a tree over backwards from its lean. A tractor will if the driver is quick enough, and drives away fast enough.

A simple method of seeing whether a tree will fall on a house – or a tractor – when it comes down, is to stand well back from both house and tree – at right angles to a line between both – and hold a pencil or a twig up vertically with arm outstretched. Adjust your position so that the exposed length of the stick just covers the tree when you sight past it. Then twist your hand at right angles so that the twig is horizontal. If the tip of the twig falls short of the house you are alright; if it touches the house in your line of vision, you are all wrong. Of course you mustn't swing your arm about if you use this method. You can measure the height of a tree like this to a foot – just mark something on the ground to the left or right of the tree where the end of your twig falls then go and pace out the distance between the mark and the tree. If there is no mark, ask somebody else to stand there and guide them left or right until they stand in the right place. This is the sort of OMCS solution to a problem that any illiterate gypsy boy will think of, but many a senior wrangler will fail to find.

Stumps will rot eventually but you can hasten this process enormously by drilling holes in the top of the stump (say, 1 every 9″) and filling the holes with sodium chlorate. After a month, if you set fire to the stump, it will burn vigorously.

Converting timber

The word 'timber' is strictly used by foresters to mean big trees only, but I will use it here to mean any wood.

It is easy to saw across the grain of wood but more difficult to saw along it. The former operation is called 'cross-cutting', the latter 'ripping'. A rip-saw has bigger teeth than a cross-cut saw, and they are set at a more acute angle. Converting a big log generally amounts to ripping into planks or squared timber. Until a hundred years ago this was generally done in a 'saw-pit'. A pit was dug, the log laid over it, one man ('the bottom sawyer') got down in the pit, the 'top-sawyer' stood on top of the log and they worked a long two-handled rip-saw vertically between them. The top-sawyer had a much pleasanter time than the bottom-sawyer, who was showered with sawdust and could see nothing but the inside of the pit. I have seen pit-sawing frequently in India and Africa and other places. It is slow and arduous, and very poorly paid.

The American colonists mechanized the pit-saw by connecting the saw up to water power and in some cases even wind power. They then multipled the blades so as to be able to saw several cuts at once. Then came the engine-driven circular saw. You can buy a circular saw for a few hundred pounds, drive it with a tractor or some other engine, and happily rip up small logs with it. Or you can buy a tractor-mounted saw. This must have its blade at right angles to the length of the tractor, otherwise there will not be room to feed the log through it of course.

using a pit saw

Another ripping machine is the band-saw. This is much used by shipwrights and wheelwrights for ripping along the grain of smaller pieces of wood.

But now a new invention has placed great power in the hands of small operators, such as the reader of this book.

That is the **Portable Chain Saw Mill**. It consists of two chain saw motors mounted one at each end of a long chain saw which has rip-saw teeth. It takes a man at each end to operate. You fell the tree and then, having snigged the branches off, lay a ladder along the recumbent trunk. This gives you a 'straight edge'. The double chain saw is mounted on a sort of sled with rollers. You lay this on the ladder, start both motors, and shove the contraption slowly along the ladder.

The saw rips a plank off. You then remove your ladder (for you now have a straight edge) and rip consecutive planks off until the trunk is finished.

The advantage of this device is that you can go into the woods, rip up a huge tree trunk, and carry the planks out on your shoulder. Hitherto you would have needed a heavy tractor, or at least six big horses, to have got the tree out of the woods in the first place, and then a timber lorry to have got it to the sawmill – and the sawmill would have charged you plenty to have sawn the 'stick' up. In California I have seen magnificent houses build by *soi disant* 'freaks' out of timber and planks that they have ripped out of the felled Douglas Firs that the lumberjacks have left behind as being too awkwardly placed. Before the advent of the Saw Mill they would never have been able to have got these huge sticks out of the forest.

An even more recent invention than the Chain Saw Mill is the **Bush-pilot Beam Machine** from Canada. It is a simple clamp that holds the chain saw nearly vertically, and is welded on to a piece of U-girder. The U-girder exactly fits over a piece of 4" x 2" timber. You just nail the 4" x 2" on top of the log you wish to rip-saw, fit your piece of girder over it and saw down the grain. If you want planks, keep moving your 4" x 2" a little further in; if you want beams, roll the log through ninety degrees and cut again.

There are several woodworkers living near my farm (one, a wood turner, lives on it) and they have such a device between them and have lowered their timber costs enormously.

Now we come to another way of ripping timber along the grain, **riving** as countrymen call it or splitting.

Some trees will rive, others will not – as anybody who has ever tried to rive elm will know already. Which is why elm is good for chopping blocks and butchers' tables: it won't split. Chestnut is by far the best tree that I know for riving, and that is why I prefer to plant it over any other tree. It is the farmer's, or the smallholder's, best friend. It splits as true and sweet as you like, you can rive it into thin, straight-grained pieces, it does not rot in the ground (for a long time), it makes the very best fence posts, gate posts, gates and hurdles.

Oak will rive, although it is harder to do than chestnut and inclined to be more knotty. It too survives well in the ground. Like chestnut, only the heart wood will survive – the outer sap-wood (white, whereas the heart wood is red) rots very quickly. But the heart wood of oak is incomparable: it is by far the hardest, toughest, and most long-lasting of European woods. Nelson's ships were not called 'hearts of oak' for nothing, and an Irish boat-builder friend of mine recently pointed out a forty-foot fishing boat which his grandfather had built, eighty years before, pitch-pine on oak. The pitch-pine planking has been renewed; the oak frames are as sound as ever and certainly good for another eighty years.

Ash is your other good riving wood. The old sheep hurdles that used to be made in prodigious quantities in the good old days when sheep were habitually kept on turnips during the winter time were mostly of ash. This was not because ash was better than chestnut, but because it was more available. I made over a score of hinged gates when I first came to my Pembrokeshire farm seventeen years ago and they are only now falling to pieces owing to rot. It is noteworthy that the ones that have been creosoted fairly regularly are the ones that have survived best. I would have made the gates of chestnut if I had had chestnut, but ash was a good substitute. Beech is another good river. Riven beech is the best wood for chairs.

Now, as to the manner of riving. If you are really skilful with an axe you can stand straddled over a recumbent oak log, up to eighteen inches in diameter, if it is fairly clean, and rive it in half with repeated blows of the axe. If you are not highly skilled, you will end up with a whole log which looks as if the rats have been at it and possibly you will only have one leg.

In the latter case, it is best to use wedges and a sledge hammer. Steel wedges are best, but when driven to it I have made wooden wedges out of a non-splitting wood (elm is best) and knocked them in with a 'beetle' (big wooden mallet or maul). But steel wedges are infinitely preferable. In the case of oak and chestnut, it is best to split the log in half first, then into quarters, and then eighths if you want the wood so small. Ash too is best treated like this although I sometimes, on the riving break, cut slices off, starting from one of the surfaces, as one might rip-saw the wood. Ash is apt to 'split out': that is, your rive breaks out to the surface and you get a short – and tapering – piece of wood. This can be prevented by skilful riving with the riving break or the froe, to be described below.

Riving Table. This is a strong simple table with a strip of steel protruding from its surface at one end – the lower end of the strip driven into the ground. I prefer the strip of steel to be about three inches wide, a quarter of an inch thick, and roughly sharpened on one edge.

You start riving the pole with a hatchet or froe, push the split end onto the steel strip, then shove the pole forward, at the same time swinging the other end of it from side to side. This is an extremely quick and effective way of riving small timber (you obviously cannot use it for big pieces – anything over say nine inches is better done on the ground with wedges and sledge hammer).

Now, you can *guide* your split in the following manner. If you see the split is tending too much say to the left, then swing the end of the pole nearest you to the left only. This will bring the split back to the centre again.

The Froe. This is a tool much used by woodmen for riving small poles in the woods. The 'chair bodgers', who used to operate in the beech woods around High Wycombe and other places, made much use of it. The illustrations give a good idea of it. A wooden club is used for walloping the back of the blade to drive it into the grain. Again, you can guide the rive quite easily by twisting the handle so that the leading edge of the blade inclines towards the way you want to go. You can hold the 'work' (i.e. the pole you are riving) uncomfortably with

riving table

metal strip

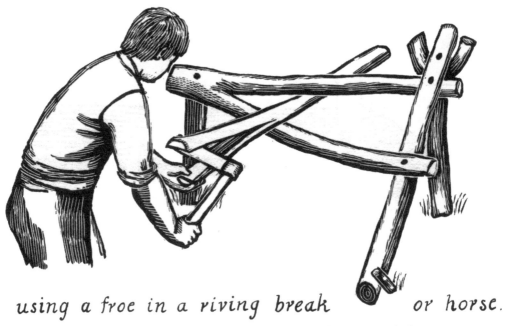

using a froe in a riving break or horse.

froe or cleaving axe

cutting edge

its lower end on the ground, but you will do the work much better in a 'riving horse' or 'break': a simple arrangement of light timber as depicted in the illustration.

Riving produces far stronger and more durable goods than ripping with the saw. The reason is that the rive follows the grain and does not reveal many torn or broken-off grains to let the water in. Sawing though has the advantage that the resulting piece of timber is quite straight-sided whereas riven timber seldom is. For gates, hurdles, fence and gate posts, and a hundred other uses (sawing horses, fence rails) where dead-straight sides and edges are not necessary, riven timber is by far the best.

Most softwoods can be split with wedges, or with the axe alone. Abraham Lincoln was supposed to have started his working life splitting trees for fencing rails and I have always supposed these were softwoods. The 'shingles' used so extensively in North America for roof cladding were made by sawing cedar or other coniferous trunks into the right lengths and then splitting the lengths with the axe. The biggest barn I ever stood in in my life – in Northern California – was roofed like this, and the walls were clad the same way with cedar felled eighty years before I saw it; it was in perfect order. But to split good shingles you really *do* have to know how to use an axe.

There are **splitting machines** (for firewood logs) on the market now. One, a simple steel cone with a tread on its surface, bolts on to the back axle of an ordinary motor car (you take the wheel off and jack the car up). You just touch a log against the spinning top of the cone and it splits it. Another, called the Impaxe Log Splitter, works by hand.

Oak plantation thinnings are not of much value (although lovely firewood) but they are often ripped down with the saw for fence posts. They then have more sap-wood in relation to heart wood than chestnut has, and are therefore, in my experience, not so good; nevertheless they are better than nothing. They are *much* better than larch or any softwood. The old way of ripping the trunks into quarters was to fell the young oaks, cut to length, then rip each piece into four with the circular saw. A quick touch against the circular saw of the ends of the quarters at a slanting angle just pointed them.

But supposing you haven't got a circular saw? It would be ridiculous to rip them down with a handsaw, so if you only had hand tools you would rive them. But new tools cause new methods to be invented, and chain saw users did not take long to invent a way of dealing with this situation. Sally's illustrations show what they do. They simply lop the top off the tree leaving a stump standing the length of the posts they want, then rip the standing stump in half (the roots holding it up conveniently for you) then rip down at right angles to the first vertical cut, then with the saw slanting and cutting upwards make four quick cuts to sharpen the poles, then slice the four quarters that you have off at ground level. One can do the whole operation in a few minutes and it is much the quickest way of ripping oak saplings into fence posts. Cleaving (riving) is still far better than ripping with the saw: the posts will last much longer because the fibres are not cut through – riving follows the grain. But if you are marketing the posts, sawn posts sell more readily because they look better, and most people buy things for looks; ignorance is bliss until your fences start falling over.

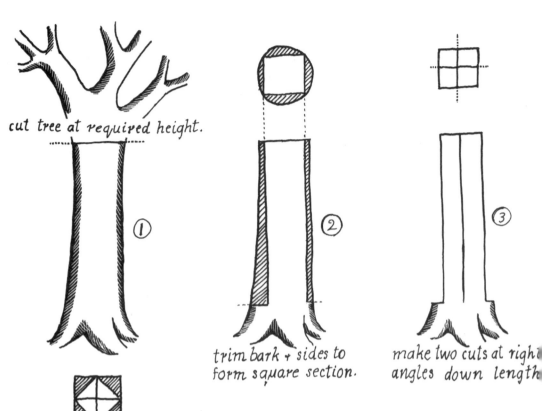

cut tree at required height. ①

trim bark & sides to
form square section. ②

make two cuts at right
angles down length ③

How to cut fence posts from standing tree.

make four diagonal
upward cuts. ④

finally, cut down
finished posts. ⑤

Heart of oak and chestnut will defy rot in the ground for half a century or more with no preservative treatment. Most other woods will not, and there are various modes of preservation. Tanalizing, which is a commercial process that involves a pressure chamber, is very good; if there is a plant near you, I should use it. Creosoting under pressure is probably just as good – but which of us has a pressure tank? The Forestry Commission may do it for you if you pay them. The next best thing is to boil wood in creosote, and *let the wood cool in it*. The last operation is most important: the boiling drives out the air, then when the wood cools a vacuum is formed which sucks in the creosote. You can easily do this in an old oil drum with the top cut out, balanced on blocks with a fire underneath it. But for Heaven's sake don't do what I did once and let the stuff boil over, catch fire, set the creosote in the drum on fire – and in my case set fire to a jeep that was standing next to it.

Boiling creosote is a dangerous process.

Boiling fence posts in creosote – *posts are left in creosote until cold & then drained on corrugated iron sheet.*

Creosoting feshly cut timber is not a good idea: the sap in the wood prevents the stuff sinking in more than a fraction of an inch. It is better to let it season first. Even then it won't penetrate far – even with boiling and cooling; pressurizing is the only really effective method.

Charring the bottoms of stakes is another method of preventing rot. We used to use it in South West Africa to defy white ants. It is probably better than nothing. Some Americans soak posts in old sump oil. They leave them soaking for weeks if they can. In fact they *store* them in sump oil. They then pull the posts out and let them drain on a corrugated iron ramp. I saw, in California, a steel tongs that had been made for the purpose of hauling them out of the bath of sump oil. After draining for a day they are nasty to handle – but not *too* nasty. I have been told that this method is much better than creosote and – in a land of a billion automobiles – free.

Firewood

A word about **wood burning appliances**. In a world in which the human population is pressing so hard against its environment it is scarcely justifiable to burn wood in a huge fireplace open to the skies. For fifteen years I burnt wood in just such a contraption and, romantic as it no doubt was, it was fiendishly uncomfortable, for no matter how raging a fire one achieved in it, nine tenths of the heat went up to warm the sky, and it would gobble up oak trees like a cow eating cabbages.

The Continentals have for centuries had far better devices. From the Alps to China you find excellent slow-combustion enclosed stoves, which are extremely efficient in generating useful heat from burning wood. The denizens of the British Isles failed to develop these because coal was so cheap that they developed coal stoves instead. The North Americans, on the other hand, drawing upon their European heritage, and ready to exploit the enormous reserves of timber that they found in their new land, developed some very good stoves.

I have installed, in the place of my huge open fire, a South African *Jetmaster*. This is a very large fire, built of sheet steel, with a heat exchanger in it. It transfers much of the heat from the smoke to the air which passes through a chamber and this heat is blown out into the room. This device is fairly efficient and on a very wooded Pembrokeshire farm I believe justifiable. But fully enclosed stoves, in which you cannot see the fire, are the most efficient of all. We have, in Pembrokeshire, a Franco-Belge, which has a big fire box, a most efficient water-heating system, a smallish oven which can be got hot enough to bake good bread, and two very inefficient hot plates. It uses an awful lot of wood but then it drives six radiators throughout a draughty house and supplies endless hot water. There are no free lunches – you do not get heat for nothing. If you want to heat a large space with wood – or heat a lot of water – you need an awful lot of wood, and be warned about it. You get nothing for nothing. The little space-heaters, of the Swedish Jotul type, are excellent for heating one room and, because they are not called upon to do a great job, can be kept going on little fuel.

If you burn wet or green wood you will produce an awful lot of tar. In the big old open chimney this does not matter: the strong up-draught of air (that first freezes the back of your neck) carries the gases away. But in slow-combustion enclosed stoves there is only the smallest movement of air up the chimney, which is what makes these stoves so efficient. Thus tar and other distillates deposit themselves in the chimney, block it up, or set it – and the house – on fire. The way to counteract this is to contrive to get the chimney *very hot*. Then the tars burn up when they are still in gas form. You can buy stainless steel insulated chimney piping. It is very expensive but in the end worth it. It never needs sweeping and is very safe. The straighter the run of the chimney the better. It is a mistake to have long horizontal or near-horizontal stretches of chimney piping in the hope that you will warm the room more efficiently. You may warm it *too* efficiently, for the thing may actually blow up. Insulated stainless steel piping as straight and vertical as possible gives the best results and the least trouble.

Probably the best arrangement for most country houses is a large and efficient water-heating and cooking stove, which drives radiators, and then a small woodburner in the living room to sit around when the weather is howling outside.

As to the best time to fell trees for firewood: in spite of many people's preconceptions, it doesn't matter a damn. Personally I never fell trees during the bird-nesting season, for I don't like to create disturbance at this time, but it is a fallacy to think that you should only fell trees in the winter 'because then the sap is out of the wood'. It is not : trees have exactly the same moisture content in summer as in winter. There may be a case in fact for felling trees in summer and then not slashing the branches off them until the leaves have dried right up: for the leaves will transpire water and help the tree to dry out. What is important is, except in the cases of ash and holly, to leave the wood for as long as possible to dry before burning it, and preferably out of the rain. And the smaller the wood is cut up the quicker it will dry.

the Woodman's grip

rope is about twice the circumference of bundle to be tied

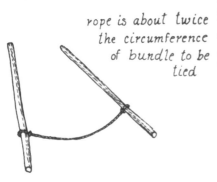

cradle - made from

sticks + rope –

- or bent pipe-

- or discarded bucket handle.

A word on **faggots**. In a world of increasing energy shortage it will soon be inadmissible to waste the **slash**, or twigs and twiggy branches, of the trees we cut down. The huge bonfire that is inevitably lit beside every hedge that is being trimmed is a huge waste. The answer is the old and forgotten faggot. Faggots are easy and quick to make if you have the right gear. This is, very simply, a sort of trough made, as in the illustration, by driving four stakes into the ground in a rectangle and joining the two stakes at each end either with a rope or, better, with a piece of bent metal. Each end piece can be made by a bent pipe and I have seen this done. The illustration makes this clear.

You simply lay your faggot material in the trough thus made and then compress the faggot by squeezing it with two sticks with a piece of cord joining them at the right point. With the leverage thus provided you can crush the twigs together very tightly indeed. You then get an assistant (or do it yourself if you are clever) to tie two pieces of baler twine (free from

ed for
ndling
faggots.

cradle

any farmer) around the faggot. Three people work very well – one to pull each lever and one to tie the strings. If you have a big stove you can make the faggots just to fit the stove and throw them straight on. They give out very intense heat very quickly. Of course they don't last long.

Tree diseases

Trees growing naturally, and in *mixed* woodland, are very hardy creatures, and normally you can just leave them alone and they will look after themselves. It is as well to note, though, that most diseases of trees are caused by fungi, and that most of the spores of these fungi cannot get entry into a healthy tree unless the living outer layers of the tree are broken or punctured. Strangely, although the tree is a living organism, the heart wood inside it is dead tissue. The tree grows outwards, and its life deserts the woody material that has been left behind by the living exterior. This lifeless matter is vulnerable to fungal attack.

Therefore do not damage the outer covering of your trees more than you have to; if you must, then dress the wounds with anti-fungal dressing such as 'Arbrex'. I have often just used white lead paint which seems to do the job very well. But cover the exposed wood with *something* – to deny ingress to damaging spores. When you see a tree with mushrooms growing out of its base (or bracket fungi) you

can be pretty sure that tree is beyond repair, its woody tissue eaten with fungus, and fit only for burning. Wind-broken branches should be cut back clean and painted over.

External diseases of trees, such as blights, cankers, rusts and mildews, should not appear in healthy trees growing on ground and in a climate that suits them. Once they attack, there is not much that you can do about them. The only thing really to do is to cut out the tree and go to the nursery and buy stock which is known to be immune to that particular disease.

To avoid honey fungus (*Armillaria mellea*), which will kill trees, grub up, burn or destroy all *stumps* of hardwood trees in the vicinity of a new planting. The fungus lives on dead wood and produces honey-coloured toadstools; if it infects live trees it produces white fans beneath the bark. To avoid white rot in conifers, soak with creosote the stumps of trees that you have thinned to deny the spores ingress. Cut out canker, or any other fungoid infection of the tree, right back to clean wood and paint with a fungicide such as 'Arbrex'.

Above all, plant trees that are suitable for your soil and climate, plant a mixture of species, and only use planting material that you know to be healthy.

Food-bearing trees

Recently there has been a great deal of interest in the idea of deriving as much of our sustenance as we can from trees, possibly in an attempt to get a little nearer to the habits of our simian ancestors. 'Three-dimensional farming' it has been called: that is, growing food up in the air as well as on the ground. It makes every kind of sense where it can be done, since a canopy of food-bearing trees, placed not too close together, provides protection to a ground crop underneath.

Examples of three-dimensional agriculture that are as old as the hills and of proven value are: orchards of big apple, pear, plum and cherry trees in England, with sheep, cows or pigs grazing on the lush grass beneath. Nothing can be more organically satisfying than this. The animals keep the grass cropped and with their droppings fertilize the trees; the trees benefit from the fact that the grass is thus kept short without robbing the land of its nutrients; the animals quickly eat up fallen or diseased fruit, thus stopping disease from spreading, and the land is put to a multiple use. Obviously if you wish to establish such an orchard you must plant *standard* (large) trees, and in our sub-standard age these are very hard to come by. People haven't got the guts to climb ladders to pick fruit any more.

In parts of the Mediterranean area there is true three-dimensional agriculture, with wheat or other crops being sown under almond, carob or olive trees. The carob in particular is a magnificent food tree, yielding up to twenty tons per acre of very high-protein pods, suitable for either human or animal consumption. The world is due to become dangerously short of protein, and carob cultivation could allay this shortage. If only it were encouraged. Further, good crops of wheat or barley, alternating with leguminous forage crops, can be grown beneath the trees.

But in Northern Europe, alas, and in the colder parts of North America, carobs and olives simply won't grow. Except for the fine tradition of large fruit orchards with grazed grass underneath them, there is very little that could be called 'three-dimensional', or 'two-storey', farming.

The trouble is the climate. Even chestnuts and walnuts are doubtful croppers in the British Isles. The oak used to be an important food tree in England, affording 'pannage', or pig feed from its acorns. In the Domesday Book each parish had listed under it *'pannage* for X number of pigs'. Beech trees afford good pannage too, although they do not fruit every year as oaks do. The ash tree too produces edible 'keys' or seeds. Certainly pigs (which are woodland animals) thrive in woodlands, and in the autumn at least can derive much of their food from the trees. In Spain we still see pigs being 'pastured' under oak trees and waxing fat, with no other food being given to them whatever. The electric fence should be making this kind of husbandry easier.

Meanwhile here in shivery old Northern Europe we are limited, in practice, to growing the temperate fruit trees: apples, pears, plums, cherries – if we can keep the birds off 'em – soft fruit like black and red currants, raspberries, gooseberries, and so on, and a few kinds of

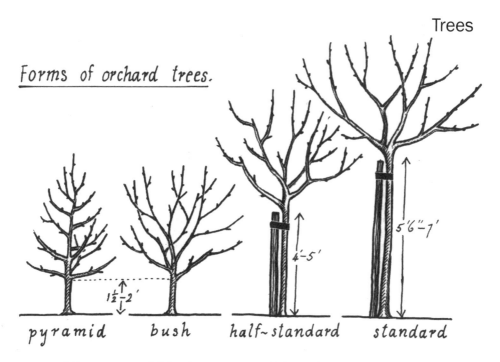

Forms of orchard trees.

pyramid   bush   half-standard   standard

nuts. The nuts could be far more useful, and provide a useful addition to our diet, if more work was done in the breeding of them. Trees of the *Corylus* genus (hazels or filberts) in particular stand up well to our climate. Hazels can make a second-storey crop, growing underneath high trees of the kind that do not cast too much shade. But the sad fact is that growing a ground crop under such an arrangement is just not possible in northern climates.

But Kentish Cobs (a cultivar of the European Hazel *(C. avellana)*) produce good nuts, can be planted, and no doubt could be grafted on existing wild hazel trees. Much good can be done to either wild or cultivated hazels by pruning the trees hard in late winter (after pollination has ceased) and then more lightly in summer to control new growth. No suckers should be allowed to grow and the trees should be opened out to the sunlight.

In North America many species of hickory are planted. These produce the excellent 'pecan' nut (or hickory nut) and it is shocking that far more work has not been done to acclimatize hickory to Northern Europe. It is shameful that we, the British, who pride ourselves so complacently on our 'heart of oak', have to buy all our good tool handles from America – to say nothing of pecan nuts! Our plant-hunters have scoured the world for useless ornamental plants and apparently forgotten to fetch home much that was not just ornamental but useful too. Now that the tide of popular taste has swung again to favour native ornamentals, maybe plant importers and breeders will be able to find time to introduce a few *useful* exotics. The introduction of *Nothofagus* (the Southern Beech) is an example of what can be done, for it looks like being by far the most useful timber tree introduced into Europe in the last couple of centuries.

As for the ordinary temperate-climate fruit trees, it may seem crazy to plant apple trees when our European partners are dumping huge quantities of 'Golden Delicious' onto our shores – so that Kentish apple growers, who can grow the most *really* delicious apples in the world, are having to leave their crops on the trees to rot. But planting hard fruit is a fairly long-term project, and who knows if the Continental dumping will go on forever? And there are few things nicer – well, in the gastronomic line, at least – than sinking one's teeth into a home-grown, unsprayed, James Grieve.

The list of poisons that are sprayed on fruit in commercial orchards now is terrifying. Our own dear old Ministry of Agriculture, Fisheries and Food recommends seven varieties of herbicide to orchard growers, all of which are highly poisonous and one of which, at least, is banned in nearly every country in the world except this one. It also recommends a horrifying list of toxins for the destruction of real and imaginary pests without which it claims that the grower simply cannot survive. Many of these are *systemics* – that is they are absorbed into every single cell in the plant's body, where they lie in wait to do their deadly work to the first insect that bites 'em.

Because so far no human apple eater has actually dropped down dead, these poisons are still considered 'safe'. I cannot forget that when I was a boy not one of these chemicals had been invented and yet apples then tasted so much more delicious than they do now! What if a few of them had 'blemishes' and a small proportion of the crop had to be thrown to the pigs? The pigs benefited and so, ultimately, did the pigs' owners and the people who ate the bacon.

So for this reason alone it is good to grow one's own apples, and any other temperate fruit. Fruit growing is a science and art far beyond the scope of this book. My own book *The Self-Sufficient Gardener* has an extensive section on fruit growing.

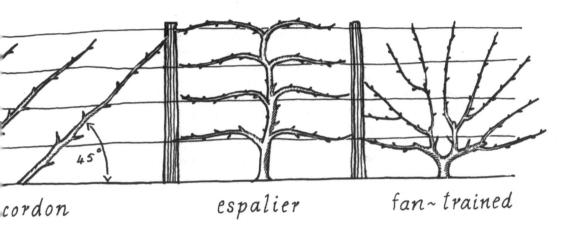

ɔrms of fruit trees trained against fences or walls.

cordon　　　　　　espalier　　　　fan~trained

Meanwhile Sally has, in her illustrations, indicated a few of the many ways in which fruit trees may be trained so as to produce much fruit in little space, so as to enhance the appearance of our gardens and pleasure grounds, so as to make the best use of sunlight and space, and so as to display the small landowner's taste and skill.

I am writing this in a small cottage on the banks of an Irish estuary. Some noble soul, long ago, had the sense to plant a gean, or Wild Cherry, not far from my window. The old tree blew down in a storm ten years ago but, before she did, she scattered a thousand seeds. These have produced a thicket of small saplings – some of them twenty foot high now – and these form, at this moment of writing, a glorious screen of soft white blossom against the deep blue of the estuary. I cannot really conceive of anything more beautiful - unless a lovely girl with black hair and a red dress should happen to walk by.

Thus we owe this enormous debt of gratitude to our forebears. We cannot repay it directly to them, but we can do it indirectly by ensuring that the same boon is handed down to our descendants.

Chapter Seven

Ponds and Lakes

This is not a book about fish farming, nor duck raising, but the engineering problems connected with maintaining, or constructing, ponds or lakes come within its brief. Whether mankind thinks of providing habitats for other creatures selfishly, that is, because it amuses us to see other plants and animals about, or altruistically, because we, being stewards of our acres, have a duty to encourage and nurture other forms of life, it is obvious that you can't have too many ponds. To any sensitive person lakes and ponds are a delight. Thoreau made the pond at Walden famous by likening it to one of the eyes of the Earth.

Making a pond

You cannot always make a pond simply by digging a hole in the ground. In many – perhaps most – places, all you will get is a hole, with some puddles in the bottom of it.

It all depends on the rock beneath the soil (whether it is pervious to water or not) and the water table. To dig a hole on top of a chalk down would obviously be a waste of time – *unless* you lined it with some impervious material. Actually many a hole *was* dug on top of chalk downs – I remember marvelling at such phenomena when I was a young man roaming on the North Downs in Kent. These are the famous **dew ponds**. But the water is retained in them by first lining the hole with puddled chalk or clay (nowadays, cement). The latter retained the water, and the ponds, marvellous for watering cattle, have water in them for unusually long periods. The name would suggest that dew provided all the moisture to fill them, but – though no one really understands dew ponds – rain probably also contributes. Certainly if a stream is allowed to flow into a dew pond, the pond fails.

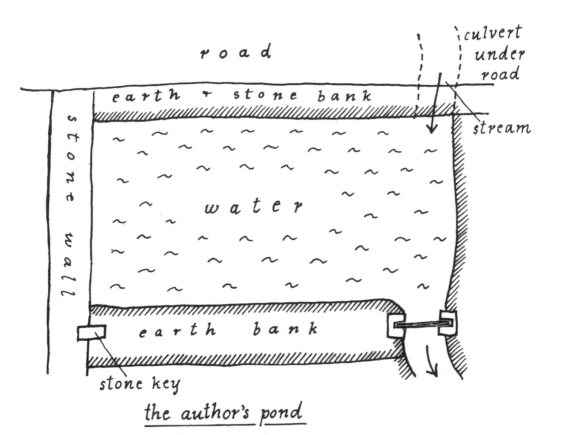

the author's pond

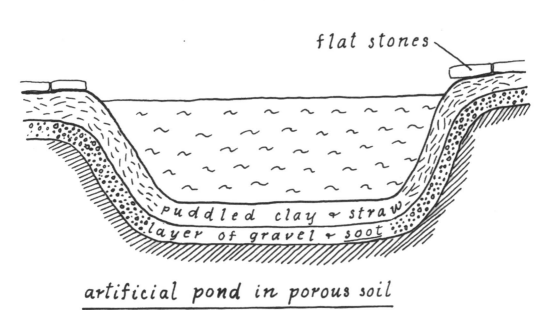

artificial pond in porous soil

If you have some flat, low-lying, swampy land, and you dig a hole in it you may get a pond. You will have reached the 'water table' and indeed dug below it. If you dig the hole in the winter you may be disappointed to find your pond go dry in the summer. If you get greedy and decide to dig an even deeper hole, you may find that your water miraculously vanishes away. You will have pierced the impervious layer (probably clay) at the bottom of the water body and simply allowed the latter to run away through pervious layers beneath.

I have a wild wet wood in Pembrokeshire and I dug a trial pit in it to see if I could make a pond there. I dug down through water and clay and then hit water and porous shale, but the water *still* did not run away. Why? Because my wood was at the bottom of a valley and the stream in the very valley bottom was no lower than the bottom of my hole. Short of deepening the valley – which probably only another Ice Age could do – I could not drain my hole. This then will, one day when I can afford it, make a perfect site for a couple of lakes. All it needs is a digging machine to dig a big pit and there will be a pond, and I can make it as deep as I like. The flooded gravel pits that occur in such profusion in the Thames Valley are examples of this. The 'rock' (gravel) is as pervious as can be but the water does not run away because there is nowhere for it to run to.

But if you wish to establish a pond in pervious rock *above* the water table you will have to line your pond with impermeable material.

Puddled clay is the ancient remedy for this.

If you take a heavy clay and *puddle* it, that is, tramp it and squodge it about, you will cause it to *defloculate*, or lose its particular structure which is so valuable to the gardener or farmer. It becomes a stubborn impervious mass – such as the potter loves. This is what you need for lining a pond. Clay, like gold, is where you find it. If you want to use it, and haven't got it on your land, you may just have to buy it. If you have to dig it by hand, God help you, because it is heavy stuff! If you enquire about, you should be able to locate some.

Dig your pond to a bit more than the required size and depth. The shallowness limit for trout is certainly the length of a heron's neck and beak. But the optimum depth for most fish farming is said to be between one yard and one and a half. Up to two yards is considered alright, but over this a 'thermocline' can develop: that is, a cold stratum of water below a certain depth which the fish will not use. If there is sufficient movement of water in and out of the pond, though, this need not be a disadvantage.

Water less than a yard deep can suffer difficulties with the water overheating in summer, and such shallow ponds can quickly become weeded up.

The sides of your pond must not be too steep – certainly no steeper than two in one. Put a layer, three or four inches deep, of small stones all over the bottom and sprinkle *soot* over this. The soot discourages earthworms, which would otherwise make holes in your clay. Puddle your clay by wetting it and tramping it with Wellington boots or bare feet. The clay must be pure and free from stones or organic material. Now tamp thoroughly nine inches of clay all over the bottom and sides of your pond. If you have an experienced driver, he can drive a tractor round the bottom. It is important that it is never allowed to dry out. Throw a layer of a few inches of *earth* into the hole and fill with water. We will discuss stocking the pond with living things in due course.

I have never made a puddled clay pond and should imagine the labour is intense, and I am told by someone who has made them that unless enormous care is taken the pond will leak and be useless anyway. He mixes his clay with chopped straw: this seems to my ignorance to be a dicey thing to do.

Concrete pond. Very expensive nowadays to make if it is any size. For a small goldfish pond a few feet or yards across it is practicable and , if well made, long lasting. If chicken wire netting is used for reinforcing, you do not need much thickness of concrete and it will not crack.

If you dig out your pond to the size you want, plus a little more, lay small stones all over its bottom (I am assuming you have no very steep slopes in it), lay chicken netting on the stones, and pour on it a mixture of one part cement to six parts sharp sand, tamp it well in so that it goes well through the chicken netting but completely covers it also (you can hook the netting up a little with a rake to let the concrete through), wait for it to dry, then skim it lightly with three-to-one 'compo' (three of sand to one of cement), you will have a very strong and long-lasting pool and one that will cost you far less than if you use the enormous quantity of concrete called for the by the average do-it-yourself manual. Nor will you need any shuttering (a wooden form into which you pour the concrete). For steep or vertical faces use dry-pack concrete: a very dry mixture (1 cement, 2 sand, 3 gravel, mixed very stiff) buttered on.

Cement is poisonous to fish and, in fact, most life, and you must scrub your pool out quite a few times, and let it soak and weather, before filling it and putting fish in it.

Flexible sheets. The only materials which seem to be suitable for this are **butylene** or **butyl rubber,** which is a newish material, by no means cheap, and has an estimated life of eighty years; although, since the stuff has only been in existence for a decade or two, I don't see how anybody can tell. For all we know it might last for ever. It is said to be the best material, particularly for large ponds. The sheets can be welded together by the supplier in any size you want. 0.030 is the gauge usually employed.

Polythene is the cheapest possible material. It is used in 0.010 size which is very cheap (if jointed in the factory it's dearer). Black polythene is best because it resists light degradation better, but even so, exposed to the sun, it will not last more than two or three years. Protected from the light by several inches of earth, however, it is said to last indefinitely. Maybe used in conjunction with puddle clay a very good and permanent bed could be achieved.

PVC is not much dearer than polythene and considered much better. It is usually of 0.014 gauge. It will last about ten years when exposed to the sun but will obviously last much longer covered.

Whichever kind of sheet you use you must be careful to see that there are no sticks and stones on the bed on which you lay it. Ideally the bottom should be covered with a layer of sand. There must be no sharp cavities and declivities into which it is going to be forced by the weight of water and thus broken (it has some elasticity but not much); you must endeavour to cover it completely with soil, turf, or

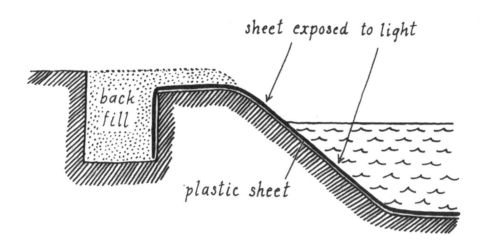

sheet exposed to light

back fill

plastic sheet

1

<u>Correct way to lay sheet for larger + more permanent ponds.</u>

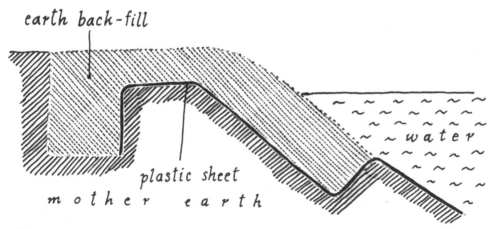

earth back-fill

plastic sheet

m o t h e r   e a r t h

it is most important that the plastic sheet should not be
subjected to the rays of the sun — all light degrades it.

2

something else to keep it from the light. Obviously the configuration in Sally's illustration 2 is better than that in illustration 1. It may seem puzzling that a flat, pretty non-elastic sheet can be made to cover an irregular depression. But wrinkles and folds don't matter. Be generous with it – don't have it stretched or very tight anywhere, keep every inch of it – above water and below – covered, if possible, both to keep the light off it and also because, as I have been informed by a Forestry Commission friend of mine, small boys just cannot resist poking sharp sticks through plastic sheets in the bottoms of ponds.

Dams are great fun to construct.

Dams have been built in the dry countries of the world to collect seasonal rains for thousands of years. In the arid northern jungle of Sri Lanka (Ceylon) there are hundreds of them, they are called *kulams*, and they are the sole support of the population. There is nothing anybody can do in a dry country more valuable than building a dam. But even in Britain and Northern Europe and North America, where, God knows, there is generally enough rain, dams are valuable.

Where we made dams in South Africa, we were lucky in that our subsoil was sufficiently impermeable not to let *all* our water seep away and the earth of which we built the dams, after hard tramping, was impermeable enough. No doubt some water did seep away into the sub-soil, but even that was not wasted, for it would eventually sur-

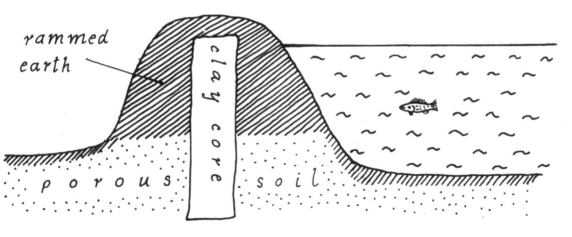

Section through dam built on porous soil

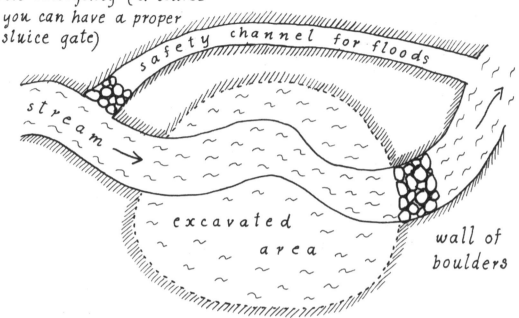

wall of boulders removed in emergency - (of course you can have a proper sluice gate)

safety channel for floods

stream →

excavated area

wall of boulders

<u>Method of establishing a pond in a stream.</u> -
- if you do not have the safety channel the whole thing can wash away.

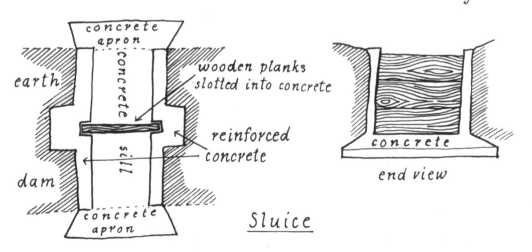

concrete apron

earth

concrete

wooden planks slotted into concrete

reinforced concrete

sill

dam

concrete apron

concrete

end view

<u>Sluice</u>

face somewhere and benefit some crop, or trees, or at least moisten the arid atmosphere.

But in England to make a really permanent **earth dam**, unless the earth is of exactly the right quality, it is safer to fit a puddled clay core. The illustration shows how to do this. Anything involving puddled clay by the way is *hard work*. If you do it yourself, your back will ache, if you employ a contractor, so will your bank balance. First you have to dig your clay, then you have to transport it, then you have to puddle it, and pack it in, and stamp it, and cover it around with earth. If there is a hole in it as big as a pencil the water will seep through it, and enlarge it, and not all the little Dutch boys in the world are going to stop your dam from washing away.

An alternative is to build either a reinforced concrete wall, as thin as you like (three inches thick with chicken wire reinforcement with some high-tensile fencing wire threaded through it horizontally: maybe one every three or four feet), or a wall of concrete blocks. Neither of these will stand up to much weight of water, therefore they must be buried on both sides with tamped earth. They must, in fact, take the place of the clay core shown in Sally's drawing. Of course, in all cases, the core must be well keyed into the sides of the valley if this is where they end. If the ends of the dam are merely brought round in a half-moon shape, so that they peter out on higher ground behind, this is not necessary. It all depends on the configuration of the land.

In most countries you are not allowed to dam or otherwise interfere with a stream of any size without asking the local Water Authority, nor are you allowed to introduce fish without asking their permission. The authorities in Britain used to be very unhelpful, but this is one of the few things that has changed for the better: they are now quite amenable. They may even give you good advice!

It is sometimes possible to dig a pond beside a stream, and let it fill with the stream waters. Sally tried doing this with a small mountain stream on the Preseli hills, only to find that almost immediately the pond silted up. The remedy was to allow the stream to run along its old course, so that all its silt went down with it, but admit water from a gap in the the side of the stream.

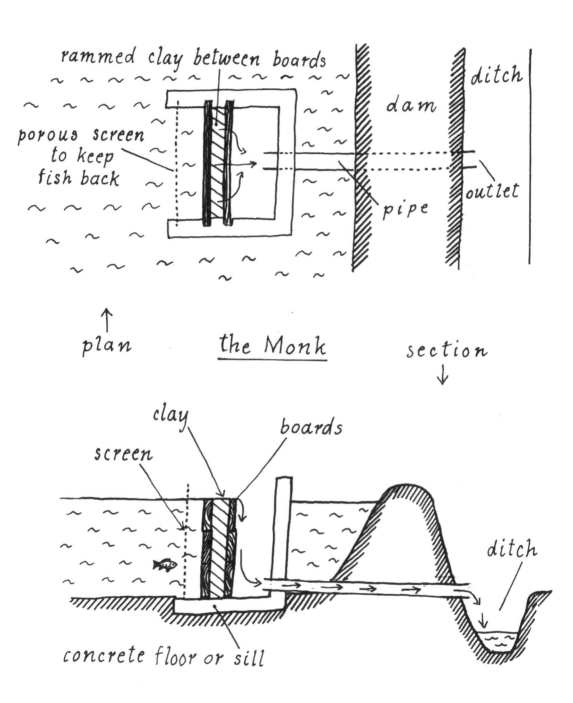

rammed clay between boards

porous screen
to keep
fish back

dam

ditch

pipe

outlet

plan

the Monk

section

clay

boards

screen

ditch

concrete floor or sill

Dams silt up. I am sorry – but they do. Either you have to empty them from time to time and scrape the silt out (and it can be quite valuable – either for concrete material, if it is sharp sand or gravel, or to put on the land if it is mud) or you have to dredge it out underwater with a thing like a dam-scraper but hauled on wire ropes, or you have to have some method of letting the water rush out from the *bottom* of the dam, in which case it will carry a lot of the silt with it.

One can fit an outlet pipe in the bottom of dams, which is a very good thing to do. It is most important, in large earth dams, that the outlet pipe should be well keyed with the clay core, or with the earth itself if this is impervious. The outlet pipe can then be opened if you want to empty the dam. If you use an iron or steel pipe there should be flanges on it to bind with the earth: if concrete or masonry, then there must be the same sort of thing.

The method used more and more for the day-by-day control of water in any artificial pond is by the use of a device known as the monk.

The monk is well shown in the illustrations. If water is in plentiful supply and you don't need to drain only from the bottom of the pond, there is no need to have *two* screens of plank with clay rammed between as depicted. One barrier of boards will do, and if there is a little leakage between the boards it does not matter. Where water is scarce, though, and must be conserved, both boards should be used and clay rammed between them. If fish are to be retained, then there should be a wire or perforated metal screen in front of the boards. If you want to draw surplus water off the *bottom* of the pool, where the water is cold, instead of the top where it is warm, it is easy enough to haul the first board screen up sufficiently and to leave the second screen in position. For this it is of course necessary to have two screens of boards. The advantages of the monk are that it gives complete control of the level of the water, enables cold water to be drawn from the bottom of the pool, and it is easy to stop fish from escaping. With an earth dam across any kind of a stream, it is advisable to have a spillway as well, to carry off storm water.

Stocking a pond

As for stocking a pond or a lake, there are many different approaches from the farm or the village duck-pond to the circular concrete tank with water being swirled round at high pressure, so full of rainbow trout that you can hardly see the water, being fed with 40% protein *at £300 a ton*.

The village duck-pond will have ducks on it and precious little else. Ducks in any concentration on water seem to inhibit or destroy all other more interesting life forms. I am not against ducks: they are the most engaging of creatures, their eggs are delicious, their beneficial association with tender green peas long established. But I prefer to see ducks on a stream rather than a stagnant pond, which, in any concentration, they quickly reduce to a stinking mess. Ducks on a large pond or lake, however, are a different thing, for there they take their part in the rest of Nature and do no harm: in fact they fertilize the water, which encourages fish. Nothing is pleasanter than to see an old-fashioned 'decoy pond', surrounded by huge trees, with an island in the middle so that ducks can nest away from foxes, with a few tame ducks kept to decoy the wild, with a keeper to throw a dish of barley into the water occasionally to keep everybody happy, and wild mallard and teal winging in from the sky – or wheeling about above the trees for their evening flight. And is it unfair if the begetter of this pond occasionally takes a reasonable toll of a brace or two to pay for his care and labour?

The circular concrete tanks with rainbow trout in them as thick as porridge I should rule out entirely. It is a ridiculous way of 'farming'. Giant trawlers scour the seas, wiping out in a few decades whole stocks and species of fish, for the fish to be pumped through fishmeal factories, carted about the globe, and finally dumped into concrete tanks to feed – *fish*. Apart from the fact that the conversion rate is deplorable – by far the greater part of the original protein is wasted – the whole thing is merely snobbism. Salmon and trout have become synonymous in the popular mind with luxury. Only *gents* can afford to catch and eat 'em. Therefore they sell at high prices and are the thing to order in a restaurant. The fact that a 'farmed' rainbow trout, force-fed and kept for all its ridiculously short life being swirled round in a never-ceasing circular stream, tastes nothing like a wild brown trout caught out of a mountain brook, or a fresh-run sea trout or salmon just in from the sea to spawn, is not suspected by the trusting restaurant customer who has never eaten the real thing. It would be better, and fairer to other forms of life, if we caught less sea fish and ate them ourselves, instead of putting them through 'battery' fish first.

But there are plenty of kinds of fish culture which are very ecologically acceptable, and which produce a valuable addition to the world sum of high quality protein.

I have a friend in Wales who dug a quarter of an acre pond on his piece of land with a JCB excavator; it has different depths of water in it down to six feet, with an underwater trench in its bottom to foil poachers (if they sweep it with a net the fish will escape below the net into the trench), with a small stream flowing into it and a spillway, protected by wire mesh, to let the water out but not the fish. He stocks it with rainbow trout, which he buys from a fish farm for a very few pennies (they will not breed in our climate very easily), throws in a few pellets occasionally, and, if ever his wife says to him: 'Go and get X number of trout for supper,' he goes out, or sends his son, an hour before the meal with a rod and line with a hook on it baited with a worm, and comes back always in time for the fish to be cooked, and always with exactly the right number of fish.

Now that seems to me to be exactly the right approach. My friend is supporting life where no life was before, supplementing his diet with a really fresh and excellent foodstuff, having some fun and providing it for his children. Incidentally American Brook Trout (*Salvelinus fontinalis*) is becoming popular.

There are plenty of semi-intensive ways of keeping fish, for example, vegetarian fish (trout are ferociously carnivorous), which are far less damaging ecologically. Carp are the traditional fish to farm in Northern Europe, and most monasteries and big houses had their carp ponds and stew ponds in days of old. People were forced to eat fish during Lent and on Fridays; they were far from the sea, there were no deep freezes, so it was either 'A plague o' these pickled herring!' or fish from fresh water. And the carp is a magnificent fish. It will breed naturally in our waters, it will get most of its food from natural

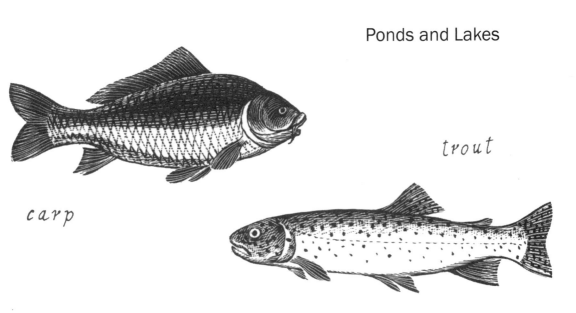

carp

trout

sources, it will cheerfully eat all sorts of vegetable rubbish that you like to dump into the water and, to my palate at least, it is absolutely delicious. The Mirror Carp is much used nowadays.

If you can provide a slightly heated pool, you are in the **Tilapia** league. In East Africa, even at coastal places such as Mombasa, where you get unlimited and very high-class sea fish, people prefer to eat Tilapia brought down all the way from Lake Victoria. Java Tilapia *(Sarotherodon mossambica),* and Nile Tilapia *(S. nilotica)* can be bought from many a pet shop, the hen fish will breed happily if kept at the right temperature, and the fish will grow and fatten at about 80°F (27°C) and will do it on food that can be provided by incubating pond water in glass-covered tanks, with some fertilizer or manure added, so as to encourage the development of phytoplankton, zooplankton and other creepies. But such intensive methods of fish farming are beyond the scope of this book – I just mention the possibilities. Stocking densities for fish farming vary enormously. Tilapia kept under glass or plastic should not be stocked at a rate of more than about two hundred fish per hundred square yards of water (ten yards by ten yards), and that is assuming the water is at least a yard deep. Trout can be kept at far greater densities – all depending on the amount of well-oxygenated water that comes into the pond and how much feeding you do. But the *minutiae* of fish culture are not really in the scope of this book. *Fish Farming* (Prism Press, Dorset, 1978) is a useful book on the subject. Catfish *(Ictalurus)* is the rage in America and can also be obtained in this country for heated ponds.

Some plants to be found in and around ponds.

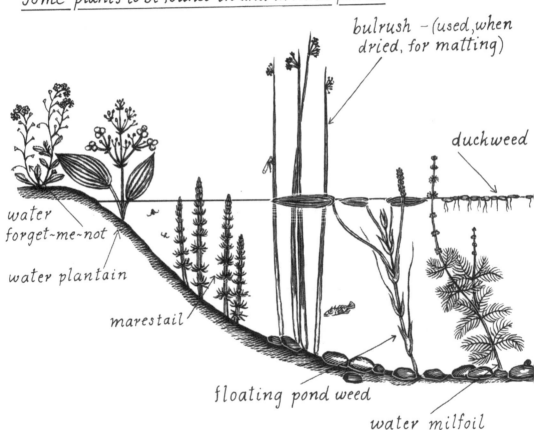

bulrush – (used, when dried, for matting)

duckweed

water forget-me-not

water plantain

marestail

floating pond weed

water milfoil

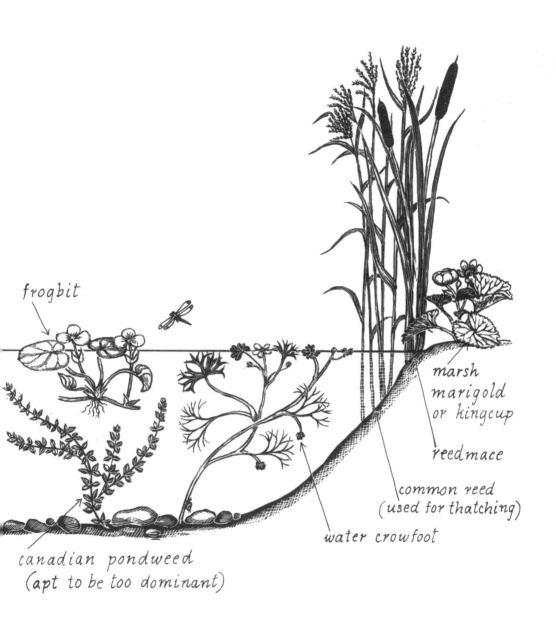

frogbit

marsh
marigold
or kingcup

reedmace

common reed
(used for thatching)

water crowfoot

canadian pondweed
(apt to be too dominant)

All outdoor ponds, except swimming pools, should have plenty of life in them. That is what they are for. It is as well to introduce plants into a new pool and, if necessary, aquatic and amphibious animals too. Various water beetles, water boatmen, dragonflies, caddis flies, sticklebacks and minnows, frogs, newts and toads can all be introduced with benefit to the pond. Any of these creatures can be apprehended by any small boy with a jam jar. Elvers can be caught with a butterfly net, in most estuaries of rivers, at flood tide and on the ebb only, at night in the springtime only. They swim upstream at such times right in close to the bank. A bucket of water with elvers in dumped into your pond will ensure eels in the future.

Plant life

When constructing your pond, make projecting bays and spits, so as to provide more water's edge, which encourages wildlife. Around the pond, some trees, such as alder, sallow and willow are beneficial and will help stabilize the banks. Trees should be kept away from the south side of the pond, so that sunshine can reach the water. Soft rushes planted on the banks will protect them from erosion.

Before planting aquatic plants, test the water for its pH value: acid water will only support such plants as Water Lobelia, Quillwort and Water Milfoil; neutral and alkaline water will support more varied vegetation. Suitable plants are such as White Water-lily (*Nymphaea alba*) and the Yellow Water-lily (*N. lutea*) for bottom rooting plants, the leaves and flowers of which float on the surface and look beautiful, Frogbit (*Hydrocharis morsus-ranae*), which floats, Water Soldier (*Stratiotes aloides*), which prefers calcareous water, Water Crowfoot (*Ranunculus aquatitis*), Amphibious Bistort (*Polygonum amphibium*), the Water Starworts (*Callitriche species*), and in fact any water plant, submerged or floating that may be available locally and which looks interesting.

If possible, use transplants, not seed, and move them at the end of their dormant period. Push them into the muddy bottom, or weight them down under a stone.

The important thing is to introduce plants of the various species needed to colonize the various zones, from the damp soil away from the edge of the pool, through the swamp, shallows, deeper water and the depths. When you fill a new pond, fling a bucket or two of pond water into it, to introduce microscopic forms of life.

Maintenance

Ponds cannot support much life unless they have a reasonable depth of clear water, are open to the sunlight and are free from decomposing matter. For this reason, it is important to keep trees back from the edges of the pond, or their dead leaves will choke the water. You will have to keep the aquatic vegetation under control, too: the Greater Reedmace *(Typha latifolia)* can, if allowed, take over and choke an entire pond. Drag the vegetation out occasionally and throw it on the compost heap, where it will do nothing but good. However, don't clear a choked pond too often, or you will disturb it. And don't clear it all at once: do one half of it late autumn or winter one year, and the next half the next winter. This will allow natural regeneration.

Try to keep the water level steady: never drain or dredge the pond completely. Cattle and sheep manure can provide too much nutrient for the water, so confine their drinking area. Also, if fertilizer or organic substances run into the pond, they will cause an excessive growth of algae.

The weeds will feed your fish (maybe going through a long food chain to do so), your ducks, and certainly your need for beauty in the world. Such a pond, full of variegated and exuberant life, is better than any concrete tank with an unhappy mixture of swirling trout and swirling water in it, the powdered remains of murdered sea fish, and nothing else.

INDEX